Prentice Hall
EARTH SCIENCE

W9-CGV-163

PEARSON

Prentice Hall

Boston, Massachusetts
Upper Saddle River, New Jersey

13-digit ISBN 978-0-13-362764-0
10-digit ISBN 0-13-362764-0
1 2 3 4 5 6 7 8 9 10   11 10 09 08 07

Contents

Since state assessments must be aligned with state curriculum standards as part of the *No Child Left Behind Act* of 2001 (NCLB), administering tests on a regular basis will allow you to monitor your students' proficiency levels. To be sure that all students will achieve success, student performances on these tests should be linked to review and practice activities.

How Does This Book Help?

The **Diagnostic Tests** help you identify areas in which individual students are having difficulty. Each question is correlated to the National Science Education Standards. After the tests, you can complete the two Diagnostic Test Reports for each student. The reports help you to pinpoint which standards students know and where weaknesses exist. The reports can also be shared. At the end of each report, there is a place for student comments, parent comments, and teacher comments if you choose to use the report as part of your communication with students and parents.

The **Benchmark Tests** will provide practice at *intervals throughout the school year* so that you can monitor each student's progress toward high levels of achievement on high-stakes testing. A comprehensive report is provided for each Benchmark Test.

The **Outcome Test** allows you to test each student's achievement level *at the end of the school year*. The test is accompanied by a comprehensive report.

The **Practice Tests** are designed to help students become comfortable with the format of the high-stakes test given *at the end of the year*. The testing uses formats and question types that students are likely to see on test day and is accompanied by a comprehensive report.

The **SAT II** and **ACT Practice Tests** give students practice to improve their scores on standardized tests.

For the tests contained in this book, there are comprehensive test reports that provide valuable information for you and your students. Each test item is correlated to the National Science Education Standards. Below is an example of one of the reports.

Name _____ Date _____ Class _____

Benchmark Test 1 Report

National Science Education Standards	Test Items	Number Correct	Proficient? Yes or No	Student Edition Chapter/Lesson
Content Standard A: Science as Inquiry				
A-1. Abilities necessary to do scientific inquiry	5, 9, 13	☐ 3		activities, 1.1, 1.2, 1.3, 1.4, 1.5
A-2. Understandings about scientific inquiry	1, 3, 4, 5, 6, 7, 8, 9, 21, 23, 33, 37, 38, 43, 68	☐ 15		1.3, 1.5, 2.3, 8.2, 8.3, 8.4, 9.1, 9.4, 11.1, 12.3, 13.1, 14.1, 14.2, 19.1, 19.3, 22.1, 22.3, 23.2, 23.3, 23.4, 24.1, 25.1, 25.2, 25.3
Content Standard B: Physical Science				
B-1. Structure of atoms	15, 16	☐ 2		2.1, 4.2, 5.1, 24.3, 25.2
B-2. Structure and properties of matter	14, 19, 22, 24, 25, 26, 27, 29, 30	☐ 9		2.1, 2.2, 2.3, 3.2, 7.1, 12.3, 18.8, 18.3
B-3. Chemical reactions	17, 18, 20, 34, 35, 41, 60	☐ 7		2.1, 3.4, 4.1, 4.3, 5.2, 7.2, 14.2, 21.3, 25.2
B-4. Motion and forces	66, 67	☐ 2		16.2, 19.1, 19.2, 22.1, 22.3, 23.1, 25.2
B-5. Conservation of energy and increase in disorder	40	☐ 1		17.2, 17.3, 18.1, 18.2, 20.2, 24.3, 25.1
B-6. Interactions of energy and matter	59	☐ 1		8.1, 8.2, 8.3, 8.4, 9.4, 16.2, 16.3, 17.2, 24.1, 24.2, 24.3, 25.2
Content Standard C: Life Science				
Content Standard D: Earth Science				
D-1. Energy in the earth system	10, 31, 32, 36, 39, 42, 61	☐ 7		1.1, 1.2, 1.4, 3.1, 4.2, 4.3, 5.1, 6.1, 6.3, 9.2, 9.3, 9.4, 10.3, 13.2, 15.1, 16.1, 16.2, 16.3, 17.1, 17.2, 17.3, 18.2, 18.3, 19.1, 19.2, 19.3, 20.1, 21.1, 21.2, 21.3, 23.2, 24.3

Test Report Title
This identifies the test that corresponds to each individual report.

Standards
This column contains a list of the National Science Education Standards that were used to develop test items.

Test Items
This column contains the list of test items that correlate to each standard.

Name _____ Date _____ Class _____

National Science Education Standards	Test Items	Number Correct	Proficient? Yes or No	Student Edition Chapter/Lesson
D-2. Geochemical cycles	28, 54	☐ 2		1.4, 2.2. 3.1, 3.3, 3.4, 4.1, 4.3, 5.1, 5.2, 6.1, 7.1, 7.2, 7.3, 8.4, 10.1, 10.2, 10.3, 12.2, 12.3, 14.2, 14.3, 14.4, 15.1, 16.1, 17.2, 18.1
D-3. Origin and evolution of the earth system	2	☐ 1		1.1, 1.2, 1.4, 2.1, 3.3, 4.1, 7.1, 8.1, 8.2, 8.3, 9.1, 9.2, 9.3, 9.4, 10.1, 11.1, 11.2, 11.3, 12.1, 12.2, 12.3, 12.4, 13.1, 13.2, 13.3, 13.4, 16.3, 17.1, 21.3, 22.1, 22.2, 22.3, 23.1, 24.3
Content Standard E: Science and Technology				
E-1. Abilities of technological design	50	☐ 1		8.4
E-2. Understandings about science and technology	50, 51	☐ 2		1.3, 4.1, 4.2, 6.2, 8.2, 8.3, 8.4, 9.1, 9.4, 14.1, 14.4, 22.1, 22.3, 23.2, 23.3, 23.4, 24.1, 24.2, 24.3, 25.3
Content Standard F: Science in Personal and Social Perspectives				
F-1. Personal and community health	11, 49, 65	☐ 3		1.4, 4.3
F-3. Natural resources	12, 44, 45, 47, 48, 52, 53, 55, 58, 62, 63, 64	☐ 12		1.4, 4.1, 4.2, 4.3, 4.4, 5.2, 6.3, 14.2, 14.4
F-4. Environmental quality	11, 54, 56, 57, 58	☐ 5		1.4, 4.1, 4.2, 4.3, 4.4, 5.1, 5.2, 6.3, 17.1
F-5. Natural and human-induced hazards	11, 65	☐ 2		1.4, 4.1, 4.2, 4.3, 4.4, 5.1, 5.2, 5.3, 6.1, 6.2, 6.3, 7.2, 7.3, 8.1, 8.2, 8.3, 10.1, 20.1, 20.3, 21.3
F-6. Science and technology in local, national, and global challenges	46, 49, 51, 52	☐ 4		1.4, 4.1, 4.2, 4.3, 4.4, 5.2, 6.2, 6.3, 8.2, 8.3, 16.3, 20.3, 21.3

Number Correct
This column allows you to record the number of correct items that each student scored for each standard on the test.

Proficient? Yes or No
This column allows you to identify whether a student has reached proficiency on each standard assessed within the test.

Student Text Correlation
This column contains page references from the student textbook that provide students, especially those who have not yet reached proficiency, with the location of material that corresponds to standards they need to review.

National Science Education Standards	Diagnostic Test A	Diagnostic Test B	Benchmark Test 1	Benchmark Test 2
Content Standard A: Science as Inquiry				
A-1: Abilities necessary to do scientific inquiry	7, 72, 74, 75, 140	49	5, 9, 13	39, 42
A-2: Understandings about scientific inquiry	1, 2, 23, 49, 56, 58, 59, 72, 76, 77, 84, 110, 118	3, 4, 10, 11, 36, 37, 50, 51, 52, 64, 69, 74, 76, 100, 107, 109, 115	1, 3, 4, 5, 6, 7, 8, 9, 21, 23, 33, 37, 38, 43, 68	8, 10, 18, 23, 24, 43, 44, 45
Content Stardard B: Physical Science				
B-1: Structure of Atoms	9, 10	7	15, 16	
B-2: Structure and properties of matter	8, 12, 13, 14, 18, 19, 20, 89	9, 12, 13, 14, 18, 20, 77	14, 19, 22, 24, 25, 26, 27, 29, 30	
B-3: Chemical reactions	11, 21, 22, 63, 73, 87, 88, 100, 105, 109	8, 16, 19, 28, 39, 67, 80	17, 18, 20, 34, 35, 41, 60	14
B-4: Motion and forces	36, 38, 39, 40, 47, 48, 66, 67, 68, 99, 108, 112, 115, 138	31, 32, 35, 59, 60, 61, 88, 89, 103	66, 67	17, 22
B-5: Conservation of energy and increase in disorder	62, 78, 102, 103, 129	34, 42, 87, 93, 94, 96, 98, 101	40	48
B-6: Interactions of energy and matter	44, 45, 46, 104, 106, 107, 111, 120, 121, 124, 137	38, 40, 43, 97, 102	59	3, 5, 6, 7, 15, 20, 21
Content Stardard C: Life Science				
C-1: The cell	79			
C-2: Molecular basis of heredity		70		
C-3: Biological evolution	79, 80, 81	65, 66, 70, 71, 73		
C-4: Interdependence of organisms	91, 92			
C-5: Matter, energy, and organization in living systems	29, 93, 125	72, 83, 84		
C-6: Behavior of organisms	90	82		
Content Stardard D: Earth and Space Science				
D-1: Energy in the Earth System	16, 17, 32, 33, 37, 60, 61, 65, 69, 70, 85, 86, 94, 95, 96, 97, 98, 101, 113, 114, 116, 117, 119, 122, 123, 126, 127, 128	5, 15, 17, 33, 41, 54, 55, 57, 58, 62, 63, 81, 85, 86, 91, 92, 95, 99, 104, 105, 106, 108, 110, 111, 112, 113, 114, 116, 117	10, 31, 32, 36, 39, 42, 61	1, 2, 4, 12, 16, 40, 41, 45, 46, 47, 49, 53, 54, 55
D-2: Geochemical cycles	15		28, 54	

Benchmark Test 3	Benchmark Test 4	Benchmark Test 5	Outcome Test	Practice Test 1	Practice Test 2
		45	3	23	23, 44, 46
11, 12, 13, 22, 23, 33, 36, 37, 47	2, 3, 38, 39, 43, 53, 54, 58, 59	7, 45	1, 2, 3, 9, 18, 24, 32, 33, 43, 37, 38, 40, 46	23	5, 23, 44, 46
					24
39, 40			5, 6, 8	2	9
18, 19, 20, 21, 42, 44, 45			4	24	1, 42, 49
1, 2, 3, 4, 5, 6	9, 10, 12, 42, 45, 48	35, 43	14, 29, 30, 42, 47	17	
	22, 23, 24, 25, 26, 30, 37, 40		43	21, 26, 35, 47	
46	27, 34, 57	33	16, 19		
25					14
25					
16, 25, 26, 27, 28, 30, 31			35, 36	13	6, 16
29, 50		6			2
26, 51, 52, 53, 54, 55				41	10, 28
17, 48, 49			39	29, 38	
7, 8, 9, 10, 24, 38	1, 4, 5, 6, 7, 8, 11, 13, 14, 16, 17, 18, 19, 20, 21, 28, 31, 32, 33, 35, 36, 41, 44, 46, 47, 49, 50, 51, 52, 55, 56, 60, 61, 62	1, 2, 3, 4, 5, 8, 9, 10, 11, 12	15, 23, 25, 26, 28, 31, 41, 42, 45, 48, 49, 50, 51, 52	3, 8, 9, 10, 30, 31, 33, 37, 48	3, 4, 12, 13, 15, 17, 18, 27, 30, 32, 33, 34, 38
14, 15		14	7, 12	1, 5, 6	26

National Science Education Standards	Diagnostic Test A	Diagnostic Test B	Benchmark Test 1	Benchmark Test 2
D-3: Origin and evolution of the Earth system	55, 133, 134, 135, 136, 139	1, 2, 48, 121, 122, 123, 124, 125, 126, 127, 134, 135	2	19, 34, 35
D-4: Origin and evolution of the universe	141, 142, 143	128, 129, 130, 138, 139, 140, 141, 142		
Content Standard E: Science and Technology				
E-1: Abilities of technological design	54, 75	46, 75, 131, 132, 133	50	29
E-2: Understandings about science and technology	52, 53, 74, 82, 83	49, 68, 136	50, 51	29, 30, 31
Content Standard F: Science in Personal and Social Perspectives				
F-1: Personal and community health	6	23, 24	11, 49, 65	
F-2: Population growth		119		
F-3: Natural resources	24, 25, 26, 27, 34, 42	6, 21, 22, 25, 26, 29, 30, 78, 79	12, 44, 45, 47, 48, 52, 53, 55, 58, 62, 63, 64	11
F-4: Environmental quality	30, 31	27, 90	11, 54, 56, 57, 58	13
F-5: Natural and human-induced hazards	41, 43, 50, 51, 54, 64, 130	44, 45, 47, 56, 118, 119	11, 65	9, 25, 26, 27, 28, 32, 33, 50, 51, 52
F-6: Science and technology in local, national, and global challenges	28, 35	23, 24, 119	46, 49, 51, 52	
Content Standard G: History and Nature of Science				
G-1: Science as a human endeavor	3, 4, 5, 71, 72, 77, 140	4, 49, 64, 69, 100, 137	5	36, 37, 38
G-2: Nature of scientific knowledge	57, 58, 59	50, 52, 53, 115, 137	5	36, 38, 42, 43
G-3: Historical perspectives	56, 71, 131, 132	50, 120	5	37, 39

Benchmark Test 3	Benchmark Test 4	Benchmark Test 5	Outcome Test	Practice Test 1	Practice Test 2
32, 34	29	20, 21, 22, 23, 24, 25, 26, 27, 28, 29, 30, 39, 40, 41	53, 54, 55, 56, 57, 58, 59	11, 12, 14, 32, 42, 43, 44	7, 26, 36, 39, 40, 41, 45
		31, 32, 34, 44, 46, 47, 48, 49, 50, 51, 52	60	39, 40, 45, 46, 49, 50, 51	19, 43, 47, 48, 50, 51
	43	36, 37, 38		28	
35		36, 37, 38, 42	11, 21	28	
	15		11		20, 35
				4	
41, 42, 43			10, 13, 17	7, 15	11, 20, 22, 29
	15			20, 22, 34	
		13, 15, 16	20, 22, 27, 52	18, 25, 27, 36, 25	8, 21, 37
	15, 18, 19	15, 16	11, 12	16, 19	
11, 12, 13, 22, 23		42	24, 32, 33, 34	23	23, 46
12, 13, 22, 23		42	24, 32, 33, 34	23	23
22, 23		17, 18, 19	24, 34	23	31, 44

Diagnostic Test A

1. Which of the following is **NOT** a subdivision of Earth science?

   A geology
   B astronomy
   C biology
   D oceanography

2. Oceans, rivers, and lakes are part of which of Earth's spheres?

   A hydrosphere
   B biosphere
   C atmosphere
   D geosphere

3. Why is the theory of plate tectonics is important to Earth scientists?

   A It explains how water is recycled through Earth's hydrosphere.
   B It explains how volcanoces and earthquakes occur and how continents move.
   C It explains how fossils form and can be used to date rock layers.
   D It explains star formation and the life cycles of stars.

4. Maps made using a conic projection have little distortion over small distances. What are conic projections used for?

   A by sailors for navigation
   B to show the accurate shapes of landmasses over large distances
   C to show directions accurately over large distances
   D to make road maps and weather maps

5. What other parts of the Earth system would a scientist who studies plants need to be concerned about?

   A changes in climate, types of soil
   B birds on another continent
   C earthquakes and movements of the continents
   D ocean salinity and currents in the deep ocean

6. How could humans cutting down a forest in a mountainous area affect the geosphere?

   A Cutting all the trees could result in a volcanic eruption.
   B Cutting all the trees could result in changes in rainfall.
   C Cutting all the trees could result in soil erosion.
   D Cutting all the trees could result in changes in bird migrations.

7. What is a scientific hypothesis?

   A a testable explanation that may or may not be supported by results
   B any accepted explanation of a set of observations
   C a well tested and widely accepted explanation of observable facts
   D an explanation of observations that cannot be discarded

GO ON

Diagnostic Test A (continued)

8. The periodic table of elements is arranged in a particular order. Which of the following statements is true regarding the periodic table?

  I. The rows in the periodic table are called periods.
  II. The columns in the periodic table are called groups.
  III. Metallic elements dominate the left side of the table.

   A I, II, and III
   B I and II
   C II and III
   D I and III

9. The three models of carbon shown below are examples of what type of atoms?

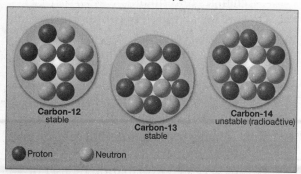

   A ions
   B protons
   C neutrons
   D isotopes

10. What type of chemical bonding is shown in the water molecule below?

   H₂O

   A ionic bonding
   B covalent bonding
   C metallic bonding
   D isotopic bonding

11. Annika did an experiment in which she dissolved a variety of substances in five different beakers filled with water. She let the beakers sit until all of the water had evaporated. She noticed that in three of the beakers, a solid had formed on the bottom of the beakers. What process of mineral formation did Annika model?

   A precipitation
   B hydrothermal activity
   C the formation of placers
   D crystallization due to pressure

12. Minerals such as gold, silver, and copper occur in relatively pure form. Another name for these minerals is

   A halides.
   B sulfates.
   C oxides.
   D native elements.

13. How would you test the streak of a mineral?

   A by scratching it with a knife
   B by looking at it with a hand lens
   C by dropping hydrochloric acid on it
   D by rubbing it over a piece of unglazed porcelain

14. How would you find the density of a sample of a metallic silver-colored mineral?

   A add the volume of the sample to the mass of the sample
   B subtract the mass of the sample from the volume of the sample
   C divide the mass of the sample by the volume of the sample
   D multiple the mass of the sample by the volume of the sample

GO ON

Diagnostic Test A (continued)

15. Which of the following processes in the carbon cycle would result in carbon dioxide **entering** the atmosphere?

  A photosynthesis of trees in a forest
  B burning of coal in a power plant
  C weathering of a granite outcrop
  D deposition of limestone in the ocean

16. Which of the following is an example of a rock?

  A a piece of granite
  B arm bone of a monkey
  C a quartz crystal
  D a piece of wood

17. What do the arrows in the diagram indicate?

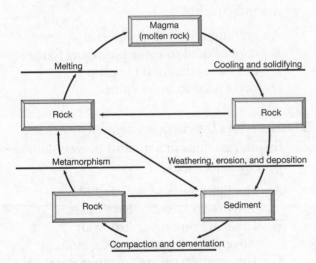

  A changes in temperature
  B alternate paths of rock formation
  C chemical composition
  D changes in pressure

18. What is true of intrusive igneous rocks?

  A They form from cooling lava.
  B They form on Earth's surface.
  C They form when magma hardens beneath Earth's surface.
  D Their formation is easy to observe.

19. Igneous rocks are classified according to

  A size and shape.
  B color and rate of cooling.
  C texture and arrangement of crystals.
  D texture and composition.

20. A group of students is examining some unknown sedimentary rocks. Seashells and pieces of coral are present in the samples. What is the proper classification of these rocks?

  A clastic
  B chemical
  C biochemical
  D oceanic

21. In which of the following situations would metamorphism **MOST LIKELY** take place?

  A at Earth's surface on a sandy beach
  B at Earth's surface in an area with a large landslide
  C in an area with high temperatures and pressures deep within Earth
  D within a cooling magma chamber beneath an inactive volcano

GO ON

Diagnostic Test A (continued)

Directions: *Use the diagram below to answer Question 22.*

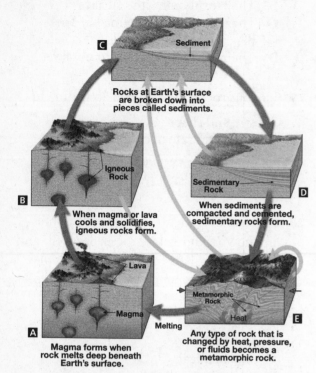

Sediment

Rocks at Earth's surface are broken down into pieces called sediments.

C

Igneous Rock

B

When magma or lava cools and solidifies, igneous rocks form.

Sedimentary Rock

D

When sediments are compacted and cemented, sedimentary rocks form.

Lava

Magma

A

Melting

Metamorphic Rock

Heat

E

Any type of rock that is changed by heat, pressure, or fluids becomes a metamorphic rock.

Magma forms when rock melts deep beneath Earth's surface.

22. Which processes in the diagram are most closely associated with mountain building and plate tectonics?

A processes A and B
B processes C and D
C processes A, B, and E
D processes C, D, and E

23. What is true of nonfoliated metamorphic rocks?

A They are usually made up of many minerals.
B They have a banded texture.
C They do not have a layered appearance.
D They do not have large, interlocking crystals.

24. Which of following is an example of a renewable resource?

A iron ore used to make steel
B petroleum used in cars and trucks
C coal burned to make electricity
D cotton used to make clothing

25. Which energy resource in North America may provide a new source of petroleum-based fuels?

A oil shale and tar sands
B geothermal wells
C uranium ore
D hydroelectric dams

26. Which of the following is an example of a nonmetallic mineral resource used in manufacturing?

A gold used in making jewelry
B copper used to make plumbing fixtures
C quartz used in making glass
D silver used to make coins

27. How does the energy generated by nuclear fission reactions in a nuclear power plant generate electricity?

A The light released is collected by mirrors and used to heat water.
B The reaction causes strong air movements which drive turbines.
C The reaction causes an explosion which generates heat and light.
D The heat released by the nuclear reaction drives steam turbines.

GO ON

Diagnostic Test A (continued)

28. The Glen Canyon Dam on the Colorade River in Arizona provides electricity for people in the surrounding area. What is the source of energy at this site?

A geothermal energy
B hydroelectric power
C tidal power
D wind energy

29. Why is ozone in the upper atmosphere important to life on Earth?

A It causes air pollution and breathing problems.
B It causes global warming.
C It protects organisms from harmful ultaviolet radiation.
D It is important in the process of photosynthesis in plants.

30. In the 1970s, a large number of sewage treatment plants were constructed to reduce the discharge of untreated sewage into rivers, lakes, and bays. What environmental law passed by the U.S. Congress required this increased activity?

A 1972 Clean Water Act
B 1974 Safe Drinking Water Act
C 1970 Clean Air Act
D 1976 Resource Conservation and Recovery Act

31. How does the recycling of paper, aluminum cans, glass bottles, and plastic bottles help to protect land resources?

A It results in the construction of more modern sanitary landfills.
B It conserves resources and prevents useful items from filling up landfills.
C It results in the need for more mining and the cutting of more trees.
D It causes soil erosion and pollution of groundwater resources.

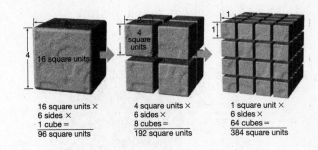

16 square units ×
6 sides ×
1 cube =
96 square units

4 square units ×
6 sides ×
8 cubes =
192 square units

1 square unit ×
6 sides ×
64 cubes =
384 square units

32. According to the diagram above, mechanical weathering

A takes many years to accomplish.
B increases a rock's surface area.
C is caused by the expansion of ice.
D protects the inner sections of rock.

33. Which of the following areas would experience the fastest rates of chemical weathering?

A a warm and dry desert area
B a cold and dry mountain area
C a warm and moist area near a coast
D a cold and moist mountain area

Diagnostic Test A

GO ON

Diagnostic Test A (continued)

34. The A horizon contains a mixture of

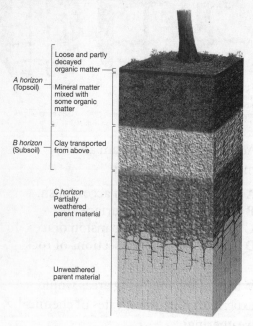

A horizon (Topsoil)
- Loose and partly decayed organic matter
- Mineral matter mixed with some organic matter

B horizon (Subsoil)
- Clay transported from above

C horizon
Partially weathered parent material

Unweathered parent material

A weathered parent material and organic matter.

B mineral matter and unweathered parent material.

C clay and decayed organic matter.

D mineral matter and organic matter.

35. Which of the following human activities would **MOST LIKELY** result in the highest rates of soil erosion?

A selectively cutting trees in a forest

B planting crops in rows that follow the land contours

C planting crops in terraces on steeper slopes

D clear-cut logging on steep mountain slopes

36. A forest fire in a hilly area destroyed the vegetation on the slopes surrounding a small town. A strong thunderstorm brought heavy rains which helps put out the fire. Should the town be prepared for the possibility of mass movements?

A Yes, mudslides could be triggered by the hot winds from the fires.

B No, the forest fires helped to stabilize the slopes.

C Yes, mudslides could be triggered by the heavy rains on the slopes where the fires removed vegetation.

D No, the removal of vegetation by the fires helps to prevent mudslides.

37. The diagram shows the movement of water in the water cycle. Based upon the diagram, which of the following is likely to happen to pesticides in the soil?

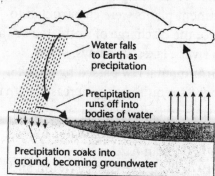

Water falls to Earth as precipitation

Precipitation runs off into bodies of water

Precipitation soaks into ground, becoming groundwater

A They will stay in the soil.

B They will evaporate into the air.

C They will run off into bodies of water.

D They will disappear from the Earth.

38. Which of the following streams should be able to erode and transport the most material?

A a curving stream with a low gradient

B a curving stream with a moderate gradient

C a straight stream with a low gradient

D a straight stream with a steep gradient

GO ON

Diagnostic Test A (continued)

39. What is the ultimate base level of a river?

    A where the river joins another river
    B where the river joins the ocean
    C where the river joins a large lake
    D the highest point on the river bank

40. Deposition occurs in streams as

    A the water flow increases in speed.
    B the velocity of the stream decreases.
    C the stream profile drops rapidly.
    D the sediment becomes too heavy.

41. Which of the following events could cause a major flood?

    A a major drought which results in a decrease in river discharge
    B construction of a flood-control dam
    C the failure of an artifical levee after a long period of heavy rains
    D the reinforcement of the artifical levees along the river

42. How can salt applied to roads in the winter contaminate groundwater supplies?

    A Salt is dissolved by rain and percolates down through the ground to the water table
    B Salt blows into rivers and travels to the ocean
    C Salt is dissolved and runs off into stream and rivers
    D Salt is deposited in sedimentary rocks during floods

43. What type of bedrock is commonly found in areas with karst landforms?

    A granite
    B sandstone
    C marble
    D limestone

44. Some of the valleys in Yosemite National Park in California are hanging valleys with spectacular waterfalls. Hanging valleys form

    A when rivers carve V-shaped valleys into bedrock.
    B as the result of erosion by valley glaciers.
    C as the result of deflation and abrasion by wind.
    D as continental ice sheets scour the land.

45. Where on Earth are ice sheets currently found?

    A in the Rocky Mountains
    B in Antarctica
    C in the Himalayas
    D in the Alps

46. According to the diagram of subsurface water features, the feature labeled C is

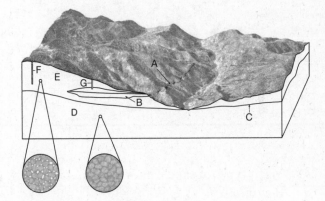

    A the main water table.
    B an aquitard.
    C the zone of aeration.
    D an artesian well.

GO ON

Diagnostic Test A (continued)

47. What is responsible for most of the erosion in deserts such as California's Mojave and Colorado Deserts?

  A ice
  B chemical weathering
  C wind
  D running water

48. What are the two main ways that wind causes erosion in deserts?

  A evaporation and soil infiltration
  B plucking and abrasion
  C deposition and plucking
  D abrasion and deflation

Directions: *Use the diagram below to answer Question 49.*

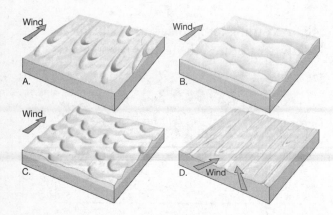

49. What types of sand dunes are illustrated in diagram A?

  A barchan dunes
  B transverse dunes
  C longitudinal dunes
  D parabolic dunes

50. The area within Earth where an earthquake starts is called

  A the fault.
  B the epicenter.
  C the focus.
  D the eye.

51. A smaller earthquake that occurs several days after a major earthquake is known as

  A a foreshock.
  B a surface quake.
  C a tsunamis.
  D an aftershock.

52. Earthquake magnitude, as measured on the Richter scale, is based on

  A the amount of damage done by an earthquake.
  B the amplitude of an earthquake's seismic waves.
  C the modified Mercalli value of an earthquake.
  D the number of people who can feel the earthquake.

53. What data is needed in order to locate the epicenter of an earthquake?

  A travel-time graphs for three or more seismographs
  B Richter magnitudes from three or more seismographs
  C moment magnitude data from three or more seismographs
  D travel-time graphs for two seimographs

54. Which of the following would **NOT** reduce the damage caused by a major earthquake?

  A installing automatic shut-off values in gas lines
  B reinforcing and bolting walls to foundations in wood-frame houses
  C construction of tall nonreinforced brick buildings
  D construction of tall buildings with base-isolators

GO ON

Diagnostic Test A (continued)

55. What does the outer core of Earth consist of?

    A liquid layer of iron-nickel alloy
    B layer of the rock peridotite
    C solid layer of iron-nickel alloy
    D layer of granite

56. What is the hyposthesis of continental drift?

    A A hypothesis that states that the continents were once connected by land bridges.
    B A hypothesis that states the the continents were once joined in a single supercontinent.
    C A hypothesis that states that new lithosphere is created at mid-ocean ridges.
    D A hypothesis that states that the plates move due to convection currents in the mantle.

57. What caused most scientists to reject Wegener's hypothesis of continental drift?

    A His fossil evidence was incorrect.
    B He could not describe a mechanism for the movement of the continents.
    C His climate evidence was incorrect.
    D He could not find matching rock types and structures across ocean basins.

58. How are the processes of sea-floor spreading and subduction related?

    A The oldest sea floor was formed by sea-floor spreading in subduction zones and the youngest sea floor is formed by subduction at mid-ocean ridges.
    B Sea-flooring spreading occurs at both mid-ocean ridges and in subduction zones forming new sea floor.
    C New sea floor is formed by sea-floor spreading at mid-ocean ridges and old sea floor is destroyed in subduction zones.
    D New sea floor is formed by sea-flooring spreading at subduction zones and old sea floor is destroyed at mid-ocean ridges.

59. Which of the following is **NOT** evidence of plate tectonics?

    A the increase in the age of ocean crust with distance from a ridge
    B the magnetic patterns on either side of a mid-ocean ridge
    C the vertical distribution of marine organisms
    D the existence of deep-sea trenches on the ocean floor

GO ON

Diagnostic Test A (continued)

60. What feature is labeled G in this diagram of an oceanic-continental convergent boundary?

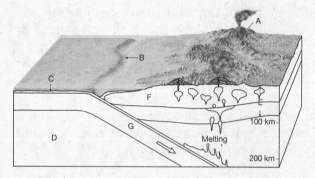

- **A** a trench
- **B** upwarping
- **C** the asthenosphere
- **D** a subduction zone

61. What is the ultimate force that drives the mechanisms of slab-pull and ridge-push in plate tectonics?

- **A** expansion of hot mantle plumes
- **B** energy from the sun
- **C** the rotation of Earth
- **D** gravity

62. What effect does pressure have on the melting point of rock deep within Earth?

- **A** Pressure has no effect on the melting point of rock
- **B** Increased pressure will decrease the melting point of rock
- **C** Increased pressure will increase the melting point of rock
- **D** Decreased pressure will increase the melting point of rock

63. The major factors that determine whether a volcano erupts explosively or quietly are

- **A** magma composition, height of the volcano, and magma temperature.
- **B** magma composition, magma temperature, and amount of dissolved gases in the magma.
- **C** magma color, magma composition, and magma temperature.
- **D** magma composition, amount of dissolved gases in the magma, and time of year.

64. What determines the shape of a volcanic cone?

- **A** the type of rock on which the volcano forms
- **B** the type of material ejected by the volcano
- **C** the size of the opening from which the lava flows
- **D** the length of the central vent

65. Which of the intrusive igneous features shown in the diagram are formed when magma intrudes parallel to layers of sedimentary rock to form a mainly horizontal feature?

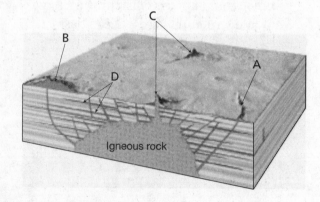

- **A** dikes
- **B** laccoliths
- **C** volcanic necks
- **D** sills

GO ON

Diagnostic Test A (continued)

66. A variety of rock types are found in an area that has undergone deformation. Which of the following rock types in the area is **MOST LIKELY** to become ductile as a result of deformation?

   A rock salt
   B granite
   C limestone
   D basalt

67. When most mountain ranges are formed by tectonic processes, Earth's crust is shortened and thickened. What is the process called where the crustal thickness changes to establish a gravitational balance?

   A compressional stress
   B tensional stress
   C isostatic adjustment
   D shear stress

68. The diagram below shows an example of which type of fault?

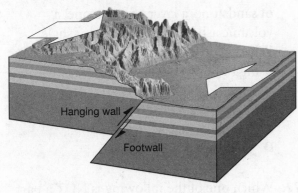

   A thrust
   B normal
   C reverse
   D strike-slip

69. Basins are large, roughly circular structures formed by the downwarping of rock layers. What would be the pattern of age relationships for the sedimentary rock layers in a basin?

   A Rock layers would form a circular pattern with the rock ages the same everywhere.
   B Rock layers would form a circular pattern with the youngest rocks in the center and older rocks along the edges.
   C Rock layers would form a circular pattern with the oldest rocks in the center and the youngest rocks along the edges.
   D Rock layers would form a pattern of parallel ridges with the oldest rocks in the center and the youngest rocks along the edge.

70. Which mountain type forms at divergent plate boundaries along ocean ridges?

   A folded mountains
   B fault-block mountains
   C dome mountains
   D volcanic mountains

71. How have scientists determined what Earth was like shortly after it formed?

   A by studying the surfaces of the other inner planets
   B by studying some of the moons of other planets
   C by studying Earth's moon
   D all of the above

GO ON

Name _____ Date _____ Class _____

Diagnostic Test A (continued)

72. What is the age relationship between the batholith, dike B, dike A, and the sill?

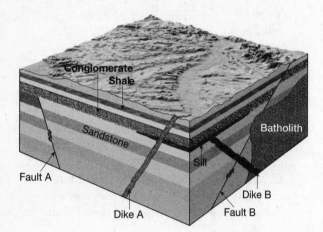

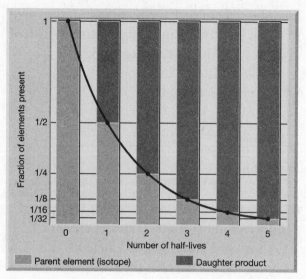

A They are all approximately the same age.

B The batholith is much younger than the other units.

C The batholith formed first, followed by the sill and dike B, followed by the formation of dike A.

D The sill and the batholith are the same age and are much younger than both dike B and dike A.

73. Which of the following organisms is **MOST** likely to have at least some of its body parts preserved as a fossil?

A a clam
B a worm
C a jellyfish
D a tree leaf

74. A sedimentary rock unit contained fossils from a small carnivorous mammal, an herbivorous mammal, and grass pollen. What type of ancient environment does this rock unit **MOST** likely represent?

A prairie-like land environment
B shallow tropical ocean environment
C cold, polar land environment
D deep-ocean environment

75. Use the graph to determine what fraction of the parent element remains after four half-lives.

A one-half
B one-quarter
C one-eighth
D one-sixteenth

76. A sequence of rock layers consists of a layer of sandstone, a layer of limestone, a volcanic ash layer, and a layer of shale. Which of these rock layers can be dated using radiometric dating methods?

A limestone layer
B volcanic ash layer
C sandstone layer
D shale layer

77. Which one of the following is **NOT** a part of the geologic time scale?

A eras
B eons
C epochs
D endpoints

Diagnostic Test A

GO ON

Diagnostic Test A (continued)

78. How did the early Earth differ from our planet today?

  A Early Earth was molten and gradually cooled to form a rocky sphere.

  B Early Earth was made of icy matter that collected to form a sphere.

  C Early Earth had the same composition as Saturn's moon, Titan.

  D Early Earth was gaseous and gradually formed a solid sphere.

79. Earth's early atmosphere had no oxygen. How did this gas become a critical part of our modern atmosphere?

  A It was transported to Earth with radiation from the sun.

  B It was given off as a by-product of photosynthesis.

  C It formed as carbon combined with other elements.

  D It was erupted by volcanoes shortly after Earth formed.

80. Why were reptiles the dominant land animal for more than 160 million years?

  A They developed wings.

  B They easily adapted to cold climates.

  C Their tough skin protected them against predators.

  D Their shelled egg eliminated a water dwelling stage.

81. Which group replaced reptiles as the dominant land life?

  A birds

  B trilobites

  C mammals

  D invertebrates

82. Approximately what percentage of Earth's surface is covered by the oceans?

  A about 35%

  B about 50%

  C about 71%

  D about 93%

83. Which of the following statement is **NOT** true about the topography of the ocean floor?

  A The ocean floor is flat, there are no mountain ranges on the ocean floor.

  B The ocean floor has many of the same topographic features seen on land.

  C The topographic features of the ocean floor include deep trenches, high mountain ranges, and flat regions.

  D Large submarine plateaus can be found in some areas of the ocean floor.

84. Which of the following features marks a long system of mountain ranges on the ocean floor?

  A ocean plateaus

  B mid-ocean ridges

  C ocean trenches

  D guyots

85. How do deep-ocean trenches form?

  A excessive erosion resulting from turbidity currents

  B earthquake activity and faulting resulting in large cracks on the ocean floor

  C plate tectonic activity and subduction of one plate beneath another

  D seafloor spreading at divergent plate boundaries

GO ON ⟩

Diagnostic Test A (continued)

86. What type of ocean floor sediment would most likely be found in an area where evaporation is high?

  A manganese nodules
  B salts
  C calcium carbonates
  D calcareous ooze

87. Most oceanic gas hydrates such as those off the northern California coast are created when

  A drilling takes place offshore.
  B warm ocean currents are trapped.
  C bacteria break down organic matter.
  D pollutants are released into the ocean.

88. What general conclusion can be made from the graph?

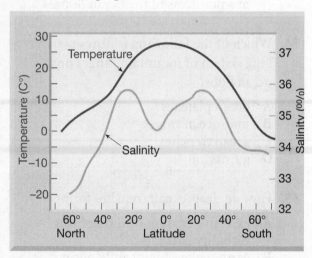

  A elevated temperatures = lower salinity
  B elevated salinity = lower temperatures
  C elevated salinity = constant temperature
  D elevated temperature = elevated salinity

89. Based on the data shown in these two graphs below, what causes the surface water temperature to differ so dramatically?

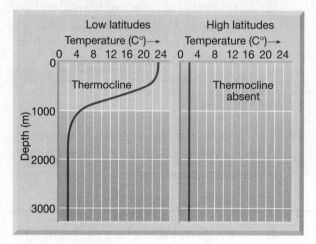

  A ocean currents
  B solar radiation
  C salinity
  D density

90. How would a shark that lives in a shallow tropical ocean be classified?

  A benthos
  B zooplankton
  C phytoplankton
  D nekton

91. Why do benthic organisms, such as algae or seaweed, only live in shallow areas of the oceans?

  A They can only live in shallow areas where the temperature is high all year.
  B They use photosynthesis to obtain food, so they need to live in shallow water where sunlight can penetrate.
  C They can only live in shallow areas where the salinity is low enough during the summer.
  D They can only live in shallow areas where sunlight cannot penetrate, so they are protected from predators.

GO ON

Diagnostic Test A (continued)

92. What factors affect oceanic photosynthetic productivity?

    I. nutrient availability
    II. solar energy availability
    III. salinity variations
    IV. changes in water temperature

    A I and II
    B II and III
    C I, II, and III
    D I, II, III, and IV

Directions: *Use the diagram below to answer Question 93.*

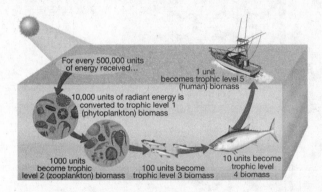

For every 500,000 units of energy received...
1 unit becomes trophic level 5 (human) biomass
10,000 units of radiant energy is converted to trophic level 1 (phytoplankton) biomass
1000 units become trophic level 2 (zooplankton) biomass
100 units become trophic level 3 biomass
10 units become trophic level 4 biomass

93. What term BEST describes the relationships in this diagram?

    A predator-prey
    B food web
    C food chain
    D trophic level chain

94. Gyres in the Northern Hemisphere flow in the opposite direction of gyres in the Southern Hemisphere because of

    A the West Wind drift.
    B the Coastal Upwelling effect.
    C the Coriolis effect.
    D the Conveyor Belt effect.

95. Upwelling along California's coast is important because it

    A causes cool winds to travel to coastal areas.
    B causes warm winds to travel to coastal areas.
    C washes away dead fish and debris from coastal areas.
    D supports large populations of fish in coastal areas.

96. Most ocean waves obtain their energy and motion from

    A wind.
    B currents.
    C Earth's rotation.
    D underwater temperatures.

97. The process by which energy moves through the water in a wave is called

    A universal orbital motion.
    B circular orbital motion.
    C universal wavelength motion.
    D circular wavelength motion.

98. Waves affect a shoreline by

    A transporting sediment to and from the shore.
    B abrading the land with the sediment they carry.
    C depositing sediment when they lose energy.
    D all of the above.

GO ON

Diagnostic Test A (continued)

99. The baymouth bar on Martha's Vineyard is a

A bar of concrete that was built to protect the bay.
B bar of rock carved out by waves.
C bar formed by sediment at the mouth of a river.
D sandbar that crosses the bay from one side to the other.

100. The ozone layer in Earth's upper atmosphere is crucial to life because it

A enhances the beneficial effects of the sun's rays.
B prevents toxic gases in the air from reaching the surface of Earth.
C protects Earth's surface from ultraviolet radiation from the sun.
D enhances the movement of nitrogen to the surface of Earth.

101. Both weather and climate are the result of

A average annual rainfall.
B average annual temperature ranges.
C frequency of wet years compared to dry years.
D energy transfer into and out of the atmosphere.

102. What is the energy transferred from one object to another due to differences in their temperatures?

A temperature
B convection
C radiation
D heat

103. According to the diagram below, which atmosphere layer has the highest temperatures?

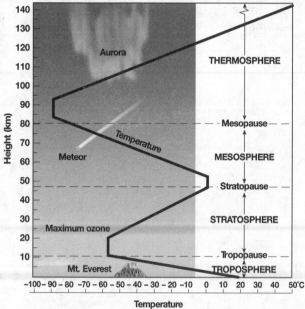

A troposphere
B mesosphere
C stratosphere
D thermosphere

104. How is the heating of a land surface different from the heating of water?

A Land heats more rapidly and cools more rapidly than water
B Land heats more slowly and cools more rapidly than water
C Land heats more slowly and cools more slowly than water
D Land heats more slowly and cools more slowly than water

GO ON

Diagnostic Test A (continued)

105. Which gas plays the biggest role in atmospheric processes?

    A nitrogen
    B hydrogen
    C carbon dioxide
    D water vapor

Directions: *Use the table below to answer Questions 106 and 107.*

Water Vapor Needed for Saturation		
Temperature		**Water Vapor Content at Saturation (g/kg)**
°C	(°F)	
−40	(−40)	0.1
−30	(−22)	0.3
−20	(−4)	0.75
−10	(14)	2
0	(32)	3.5
5	(41)	5
10	(50)	7
15	(59)	10
20	(68)	14
25	(77)	20
30	(86)	26.5
35	(95)	35
40	(104)	47

106. The number of grams of water vapor required to saturate a kilogram of air

    A increases as temperature decreases.
    B increases as temperature increases.
    C remains the same at all temperatures.
    D averages 5 grams per 5 degrees of temperature.

107. When the water-vapor content of air remains constant, lowering air temperature

    A causes a decrease in relative humidity.
    B causes an increase in relative humidity.
    C has no effect on the relative humidity.
    D causes great fluctuations in relative humidity.

108. What often occurs as air goes up a mountain slope?

    A Masses of warm air and cold air collide.
    B Localized convective lifting produces thermals.
    C The air cools, generating clouds and precipitation.
    D The air is heated, generating clouds and precipitation.

109. In the atmosphere, the process of condensation begins when rising air reaches its

    A freezing point.
    B melting point.
    C evaporation point.
    D dew point.

110. What is fog?

    A a very thin cloud that forms around mountain peaks
    B a cloud with its base at or very near the ground surface
    C a cloud that forms only at night
    D a cloud with its base between 2000 and 6000 meters from the surface

GO ON

Diagnostic Test A (continued)

111. The type of precipitation that reaches Earth's surface depends upon the

   A volume of water vapor in the lower atmosphere.

   B temperature profile in the lower few kilometers of the atmosphere.

   C presence of fog in the lower atmosphere.

   D temperature profile in the highest levels of the atmosphere.

112. The air pressure pushing down on an object

   A is heavier than the air pressure pushing up on the object.

   B exactly balances the air pressure pushing up on the object.

   C is lighter than the air pressure pushing up on the object.

   D has no effect upon the object.

113. Wind is created when air flows

   A from areas of higher pressure to areas of lower pressure.

   B from areas of lower pressure to areas of higher pressure.

   C through areas of consistent pressure.

   D from desert areas to mountain areas.

114. As a result of the Coriolis effect, wind in pressure centers in the Northern Hemisphere blow

   A counterclockwise around a low and clockwise around a high.

   B clockwise around a low and counterclockwise around a high.

   C inward around an anticyclone.

   D outward around a cyclone.

115. How does air flow around a cyclone in the Northern and Southern Hemispheres?

   A In either hemisphere the air flows outward around a cyclone.

   B In the Northern Hemisphere the air flows inwards around a cyclone, and outward in the Southern Hemisphere.

   C In the Northern Hemisphere the air flows outward around a cyclone, and inward in the Southern Hemisphere.

   D In either hemisphere the air flows inward around a cyclone.

116. What is a land breeze?

   A a nighttime breeze in which warm air moves toward the sea

   B a daytime breeze in which cool air moves toward the land

   C a daytime breeze in which warm air moves toward the land

   D a nighttime breeze in which cool air moves toward the sea

117. El Niño events are short-term weather changes that result from

   A a change in ocean currents that produces warming in the eastern tropical Pacific.

   B a change in ocean currents that produces cooling in the eastern tropical Pacific.

   C a change in wind patterns that produces colder winters in the northwestern United States.

   D a change in wind patterns that produces warmer weather in the northeastern United States.

GO ON

118. Which of the following is a huge body of air that has similar characteristics of temperature and amounts of moisture at any given altitude?

    A   a front
    B   a cyclone
    C   a prevailing wind
    D   an air mass

119. What type of air mass would form over a cold, high-latitude land area such as Northern Canada?

    A   continental polar
    B   continental tropical
    C   maritime polar
    D   maritime tropical

120. What type of front is shown in the image below?

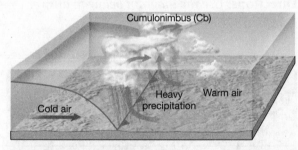

    A   a warm front
    B   a cold front
    C   an occluded front
    D   a stationary front

121. Heavy rains, high winds, cumulonimbus clouds are **most** often associated with which type of front?

    A   cold front
    B   warm front
    C   stationary front
    D   occluded front

122. Violent windstorms that take the form of a rotating column of air are

    A   monsoons.
    B   hurricanes.
    C   tornadoes.
    D   blizzards.

123. Which of the following locations would recieve the greatest amount of solar radiation?

    A   Albuquerque, New Mexico at about 35 degrees N latitude
    B   New Orleans, Louisiana at about 30 degrees N latitude
    C   Seward, Alaska at about 60 degrees N latitude
    D   Hanamaulu, Hawaii at about 21 degrees N latitude

124. The climates of coastal areas are different from those at the same latitude farther inland in that coastal areas experience

    A   cooler summers and colder winters.
    B   cooler summers and milder winters.
    C   warmer summers and warmer winters.
    D   warmer summers and milder winters.

125. How does a large amount of vegetation in an area affect the temperatures in the area?

    A   Vegetation affects how much of the sun's energy is absorbed and how fast the energy is released.
    B   Vegetation only affects the amount of precipitation in an area through transpiration.
    C   The only effect of vegetation is to increase the cloudiness of an area.
    D   Vegetation has no effect on the temperature of a land area.

GO ON

Diagnostic Test A (continued)

126. Josef has never experienced winter weather. In which climate does he live?

  A humid mid-latitude
  B humid tropical
  C highland
  D desert

127. Deserts are the result of

  A wind patterns.
  B ocean circulation.
  C mountain ranges.
  D all of the above

128. How would the climate of an area in an lowland area compare with an area nearby that is at a higher elevation?

  A The lowland area would have a cooler and wetter climate.
  B The highland area would have a cooler and wetter climate.
  C The highland area would have a warmer and dryer climate.
  D The lowland area would have a cooler and dryer climate.

129. What is Earth's greenhouse effect?

  A a natural warming of Earth's lower atmosphere and surface
  B a natural warming of Earth caused by an increase in the amount of solar energy that reaches Earth
  C a natural cooling of Earth caused by reflection and scattering of solar energy
  D an artificial cooling of Earth caused by an increase in glacial ice sheets

130. Which of the following is an example of a human activity that contributes to climate change?

  A producing sunspots
  B using solar energy
  C burning fossil fuels
  D using hydroelectric power

131. What major discovery did the Greek mathematician Eratosthenes make to the study of Earth science?

  A He concluded that Earth was round, instead of flat.
  B He developed a model for predicting lunar eclipses.
  C He calculated the circumference of Earth.
  D He proposed the heliocentric model of the solar system.

Directions: *Use the diagram below to answer Question 132.*

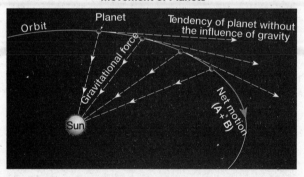

Movement of Planets

132. If the gravitational force between the sun and the planet did not exist, the planet would move in a straight line out into space because of its

  A mass.
  B weight.
  C inertia.
  D speed.

Diagnostic Test A

GO ON

Diagnostic Test A (continued)

Directions: *Use the diagram below to answer Question 133.*

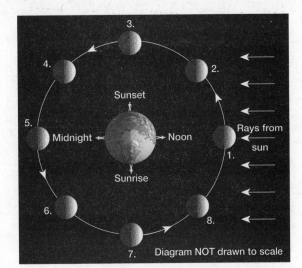

133. To an observer on Earth, the side of the moon facing Earth is dark in the first phase. In the fifth phase, the side of the moon facing Earth is fully lit. The moon in the first phase appears dark to someone on Earth because the sun's rays are shining

  A on the side of the moon facing Earth.
  B underneath the moon.
  C perpendicular to the moon.
  D on the side of the moon facing away from Earth.

134. Effects of the forces that produced the craters on our moon, Earth itself, and other planets and their satellites include

  A the generation of heat high enough to melt rock.
  B mass extinctions on the objects struck.
  C the formation of oxygen in the air around the impact.
  D all of the above.

GO ON

Diagnostic Test A (continued)

Directions: *Use the chart below to answer Question 135.*

Comparison of the Atmospheres and Surface Temperatures of Mercury, Venus, Earth, Mars					
Planet or Body	**Gases (% by volume)**			**Surface Temperature (range)**	**Surface Atmospheric Pressure (bars)**
	N₂	**O₂**	**CO₂**		
Mercury	0	trace	0	−173° to 427° C	10^{-15}
Venus	3.5	< 0.01	96.5	475° C (small range)	92
Earth	78.01	20.95	0.03	−40° to 75° C	1.014
Mars	2.7	1.3	95.32	−120° to 25° C	0.008

135. Which planet has the greatest greenhouse effect?

   A Earth
   B Mars
   C Venus
   D Mercury

136. Which of the following statements is true about Mars?

   I. Many parts of Mars's landscape resemble deserts on Earth.
   II. Mars has volcanoes.
   III. Mars has oceans.
   IV. Mars has polar ice caps.

   A II only
   B I only
   C I, II, and III
   D I, II, and IV

137. What type of electromagnetic radiation from the sun has the longest wavelengths?

   A visible light
   B X-rays
   C infrared rays
   D radio waves

138. How is the Doppler effect used in astronomy to study stars?

   A to determine the size of distant stars
   B to determine whether a star is moving away from or toward Earth
   C to determine the absolute brightness of distant stars
   D to determine the temperature and composition of stars

139. What information about a star is determined from the color of the star?

   A the star's distance from Earth
   B the star's mass
   C the star's absolute magnitude
   D the star's temperature

GO ON

Diagnostic Test A (continued)

140. Two stars of the same absolute magnitude may not have the same apparent magnitude because

    A one may be much hotter than the other.

    B they are part of a binary system.

    C one may be farther from Earth than the other.

    D their chemical compositions differ.

141. A supernova event is thought to be triggered when a massive star

    A converts to a protostar.

    B consumes most of its nuclear fuel.

    C converts all its hydrogen to uranium.

    D becomes less bright than surrounding stars.

142. Which of the following **BEST** describes a galaxy?

    A a group of starsand planets in the last stages of their life cycles

    B a large collection of dark matter that makes up much of the universe

    C a group of billions of stars, gas, and dust held together by gravity

    D an enormous collection of stars within other solar systems

Directions: *Use the image below to answer Question 143.*

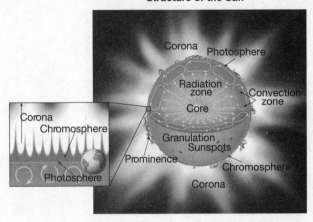

Structure of the Sun

143. Which layer is the visible "surface" of the sun?

    A solar interior

    B corona

    C chromosphere

    D photosphere

STOP

Diagnostic Test B

1. What two elements made up most of the cloud or solar nebula from which Earth and the solar system formed?

   A hydrogen and oxygen
   B hydrogen and helium
   C helium and carbon
   D hydrogen and silicon

2. Which three main layers form Earth's geosphere?

   A crust, mantle, and core
   B crust, inner core, and outer core
   C atmosphere, biosphere, and hydrosphere
   D mantle, core, and hydrosphere

3. Which labeled point shown in the image below is located at 30 degrees south and 30 degrees west?

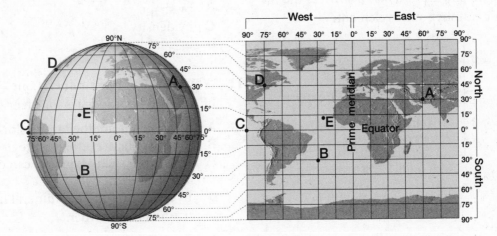

   A Point A
   B Point B
   C Point D
   D Point E

4. What feature of Earth's surface do topographic maps illustrate?

   A temperature of Earth's surface
   B geologic units on Earth's surface
   C elevation of Earth's surface
   D only the latitude and longitude of an area

5. What is the source of energy for most processes in the atmosphere, hydrosphere, and on Earth's surface?

   A fossil fuels
   B Earth's interior
   C geothermal energy
   D the sun

GO ON

Diagnostic Test B (continued)

6. Why is petroleum considered to be a nonrenwable resource?

  A Petroleum resources can never be replaced.

  B Petroleum resources take millions of years to accumulate.

  C Petroleum resources can be replaced in a few years.

  D Petroleum resources can accumulate in about 25 years.

7. Using the illustration below, what is the atomic number of this element?

  A 12.011

  B 12

  C 18

  D 6

8. What happens when chlorine reacts with sodium?

  A A green, poisonous gas will form.

  B The individual ions will bond together to form NaCl.

  C The individual ions will repel one another.

  D Gaseous halite will form.

9. Why would the concrete in a sidewalk NOT be considered to be a mineral?

  A It is not naturally occurring.

  B It is not a solid.

  C It is not inorganic.

  D It is not have a particular chemical composition.

10. How are most minerals classified into groups?

  A by color

  B by shape

  C by density

  D by composition

11. Why is the color of a mineral one of the LEAST useful properties for identification?

  A All minerals are the same color.

  B All minerals are either white or black.

  C A mineral, such as quartz, can occur in many different colors.

  D To determine color, a mineral must be crushed to a powder.

12. A mineral that breaks along flat, even planes is said to exhibit

  A cleavage.

  B fracture.

  C hardness.

  D density.

13. What is the color of a powdered mineral called?

  A color

  B streak

  C luster

  D luminescence

GO ON

Diagnostic Test B (continued)

Directions: *Use the diagram below to answers Questions 14 and 15.*

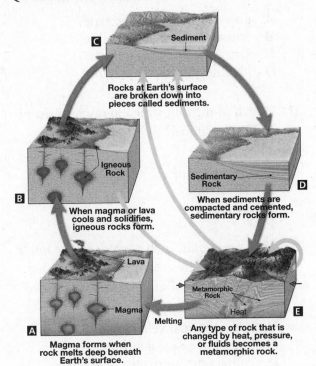

14. A rock forms as as the result of process E. What characteristic would the rock have?

   A interlocking crystals due to cooling
   B rounded pebbles
   C bands of different minerals
   D thin, flat layers of cemented sediments

15. What drives the cycle shown in the diagram?

   A energy in the atmosphere
   B energy from deep within Earth
   C the force of gravity
   D all of the above

16. Assign the following rock textures to their correct cooling history: coarsegrained, fine-grained, glassy, porphyritic.

Cooling History
A–very fast
B–fast
C–slow
D–varies

   A coarse-grained: A, fine-grained: B, glassy: C, porphyritic: D
   B coarse-grained: B, fine-grained: A, glassy: D, porphyritic: C
   C coarse-grained: C, fine-grained: B, glassy: A, porphyritic: D
   D coarse-grained: D, fine-grained: C, glassy: B, porphyritic: A

17. What is the process by which dissolved minerals are deposited in the pore spaces between sediment grains to form a sedimentary rock?

   A compaction
   B erosion
   C cementation
   D weathering

GO ON

Diagnostic Test B (continued)

18. In which type of environment did this rock likely form?

A beneath Earth's surface
B river or stream bed
C desert
D forest

19. What type of metamorphism is modeled here?

A contact
B regional
C low-grade
D heat

20. Place the following metamorphic rocks in order of increasing metamorphism.

A gneiss, schist, phyllite, slate
B schist, slate, gneiss, phyllite
C slate, phyllite, schist, gneiss
D phyllite, gneiss, slate, schist

21. Which of the following energy resources is NOT a fossil fuel?

A coal
B uranium ore
C petroleum
D natural gas

22. Heavy minerals, such as gold, can be found concentrated in stream sediments. What are these types of mineral deposits called?

A placer deposits
B hydrothermal vein deposits
C layered igneous deposits
D contact metamorphic deposits

GO ON

Name _____ Date _____ Class _____

Diagnostic Test B (continued)

23. The devices shown in the foreground provide some of the electricity used in Sacramento, California. How do these devices work?

  A They set wind turbines in motion to produce electricity.
  B They change color to indicate when solar output is high.
  C They store energy from the tides and convert it to electricity.
  D They absorb solar energy and convert it to electricity.

24. Wind power is used to generate electricity. What percentage of the United States electricity could be produced by wind power within the next 60 years?
  A 5 to 10 percent
  B 30 to 40 percent
  C 60 to 70 percent
  D 90 to 100 percent

25. Almost 71 percent of Earth's surface is covered by water, but most of this water is found in the oceans. Less than one percent of the water on Earth is fresh water. Why is this tiny fraction of the total water so important?

  A It is the only water to circulate in the water cycle.
  B People prefer the taste of fresh water to that of salty water.
  C It is necessary for the survival of humans, most other animals and plants.
  D Fresh water is only necessary for the survival of some types of plants.

26. Why is soil erosion considered to be a threat to an important land resource?

  A Fertile soil is needed to grow much of our food supply.
  B Soil erosion causes most of the air pollution in major cities.
  C Soil erosion destroys productive open-pit mining operations.
  D Soil erosion is not a threat, it creates habitat for many organisms.

27. The Clean Air Act was passed in 1970 in order to

  A protect drinking water resources.
  B establish the maximum allowable levels of six major air pollutants.
  C establish the minimum allowable levels of two major water pollutants.
  D decrease the illegal and unsafe dumping of hazardous wastes.

GO ON

Diagnostic Test B (continued)

Directions: *Use the image below to answer Question 28.*

28. What caused this type of weathering?

   A oxidation
   B the formation of clay minerals
   C exfoliation
   D biological activity

29. Soil is composed of mineral matter, humus, water, and

   A air.
   B bedrock.
   C silicates.
   D organic matter.

30. Which type of soil is commonly found in hot, wet tropical areas?

   A humus
   B laterite
   C pedalfer
   D pedocal

31. What is the major force responsible for causing mass movements?

   A creep
   B mudflows
   C wind
   D gravity

32. How do scientists classify a mass movement that consists of rocks and rock fragments that fall freely through the air?

   A as a mudflow
   B as a rockslide
   C as creep
   D as a rockfall

33. The water cycle is shown in the diagram below. Earth's water cycle is normally balanced. What would indicate that the water cycle is out of balance?

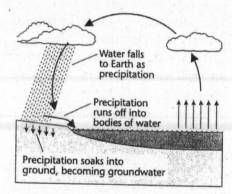

   A Evaporation equals average precipitation.
   B Level of the world oceans is not changing.
   C Level of the world oceans is dropping rapidly.
   D Amount of evaporation is higher over the oceans.

GO ON

Diagnostic Test B (continued)

Directions: *Use the chart below to answer Question 34.*

Some of the World's Largest Rivers		
River	**Country**	**Average Discharge m³/s**
Ganges	India	18,700
Amazon	Brazil	212,400
Paran	Argentina	14,900
Lena	Russia	15,500
Congo	Zaire	39,650
Orinoco	Venezuela	17,000
Yangtze	China	21,800
Mississippi	United States	17,300
Brahmaputra	Bangladesh	19,800
Yenisei	Russia	17,400

34. What is being measured in cubic meters per second?

   A the velocity of the water
   B the distance the water travels
   C the maximum volume of water that can be held
   D the volume of water flowing past a certain point in a given amount of time

35. What does the bed load of a stream consist of?

   A particles that move or roll along the bottom of the stream
   B particles that are dissolved in the water of the stream
   C particles that are too large to ever be transported by the stream
   D particles that are carried by suspension in the stream

36. The Yellowstone River valley is a V-shaped valley, which means that the river is vigorously

   A downcutting its channel.
   B flooding its channel.
   C widening its channel.
   D forming meanders in the channel.

37. Which statement is true for the Mississippi River drainage basin shown in the diagram?

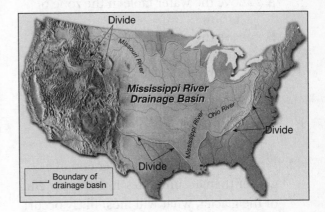

   A All the streams and rivers ultimately flow into the Ohio River.
   B Water from the entire area of the Mississippi River drainage basin flows into the Mississippi River.
   C Water from the entire area of the Mississippi River drainage basin flows into the Pacific Ocean.
   D All the streams and rivers in the drainage basin flow north into the Missouri River.

GO ON

Diagnostic Test B (continued)

38. Where do natural springs form?

  A where the water table is deep beneath Earth's surface

  B where the water table intersects the ground surface

  C where the water table intersects a river or stream

  D where groundwater is heated by volcanic activity

39. Where do most limestone caves form?

  A above the water table in the zone of aeration

  B above the water table in the zone of saturation

  C at or below the water table in the zone of aeration

  D at or below the water table in the zone of saturation

40. If more ice is lost at the lower end of a glacier than accumulates at the upper end of the glacier, what will most likely occur?

  A The glacier will advance.

  B The glacier will remain in the same place.

  C The glacier will retreat.

  D The glacier will grow larger.

41. During the last ice age how much of Earth was covered by glaciers?

  A 5 percent

  B 10 percent

  C 30 percent

  D 100 percent

42. Which of the following statements is true regarding weathering in deserts?

  A There is no weathering in deserts.

  B Most of the weathering in deserts is mechanical weathering.

  C Most of the weathering in desert is chemical weathering.

  D There is no weathering from flowing water in a desert.

43. The Basin and Range, some of which lies in southeastern California, is a desert landscape. Sporadic rains in this region often produce deposits at the mouth of canyons called

  A eskers.

  B moraines.

  C playas.

  D alluvial fans.

44. What causes an earthquake?

  A the buildup of layers of sediment

  B the elastic rebound of rock that has slipped along a fault

  C strong foreshocks and aftershocks

  D any movement along a fault plane

45. Which type of earthquake wave would cause the most damage near an earthquake's epicenter?

  A body waves

  B surface waves

  C S waves

  D P waves

GO ON

Diagnostic Test B (continued)

46. Earthquake magnitude is

    A a measure of the depth of the earthquake's epicenter.

    B the Mercalli value of earthquake damage near the epicenter.

    C a measure of the amount of energy released at the source of the earthquake.

    D the amount of earthquake shaking at a given location.

47. Which of the following would **NOT** normally be a major hazard associated with an earthquake?

    A high winds causing downed trees and power outages

    B seismic shaking causing buildings to collapse

    C landslides damaging roads and structures

    D tsunamis causing coastal flooding and destruction

48. Which of the layers of Earth's interior shown in the diagram is responsible for Earth's magnetic field?

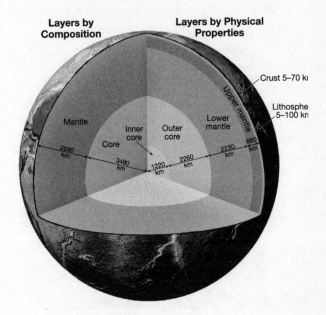

    A the crust

    B the mantle

    C the outer core

    D the inner core

49. How did scientists determine the boundaries of the layers of Earth's interior?

    A by drilling down into the core of Earth

    B from samples of rocks thrown out of volcanoes

    C from the wave paths and velocity changes of seismic waves

    D by using X-rays to obtain an image of Earth's interior

GO ON

Diagnostic Test B (continued)

50. How did the distribution of fossils of the freshwater reptile *Mesosaurus* shown below provide evidence to support continental drift?

   A It showed that the reptiles could have swum across the Atlantic Ocean because it was once a freshwater sea.

   B Since the reptiles lived in freshwater and could not have swum across a salty ocean, South America and Africa must have been joined.

   C It showed that a land bridge once connected South America and Africa allowing the reptiles to walk back and forth.

   D It showed that the animals had floated on log rafts across the entire Atlantic Ocean.

Directions: *Use the diagram below to answer Question 51.*

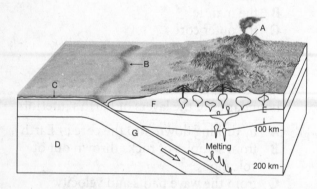

51. Identify which labeled feature in the diagram is a deep-ocean trench.

   A feature A
   B feature B
   C feature C
   D feature G

52. How does paleomagnetic evidence support the idea of seafloor spreading?

   A Mirror image paleomagentic patterns are found on either side of an ocean ridge.

   B Some ocean rocks show reversed polarity while others show normal polarity.

   C When lava cools, iron-rich minerals become magnetized in the direction parallel to the existing magnetic field.

   D Ocean floor rocks show that Earth's magnetic field has periodically reversed its polarity.

53. What layers of Earth make up the lithospheric plates?

   A the crust and lower mantle
   B the outer and inner core
   C the crust only
   D the crust and uppermost mantle

54. The driving force behind plate motion in the theory of plate tectonics is

   A heat from the sun.
   B thermal conduction in the mantle.
   C thermal convection in the mantle.
   D thermal convection in the core.

55. The Hawaiian Islands are forming as the result of

   A the Pacific Plates moving over a mantle plume.

   B the convergence of two continental plates.

   C convergence between an oceanic plate and a continental plate.

   D divergence along a mid-ocean ridge.

GO ON

Diagnostic Test B (continued)

56. What is the hotter, fast-moving basaltic lava called?

    A pahoehoe lave
    B aa lava
    C lapilli lava
    D cinder lava

57. The diagrams show the formation of Crater Lake in Oregon. Crater Lake is an example of what volcanic feature?

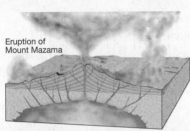

Eruption of Mount Mazama

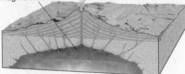

Partialy emptied magma chamber

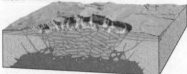

Collapse of Mount Mazama

Formation of Crater Lake and Wizard Island

    A a shield volcano
    B a volcanic neck
    C a caldera
    D a lava plateau

58. What intrusive igneous feature has a surface exposure of more than 100 square kilometers?

    A a dike
    B a sill
    C a laccolith
    D a batholith

59. What type of stress is occurring in figure D?

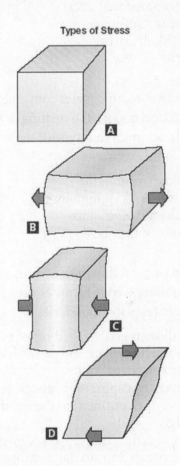

Types of Stress

    A shear stress
    B tensional stress
    C compressional stress
    D no stress

GO ON

Diagnostic Test B (continued)

60. Large upfolds of rock layers are called

   A monoclines.
   B synclines.
   C anticlines.
   D grabens.

61. What is the major type of stress involved in the formation of folded mountains?

   A compressional stress
   B shear stress
   C tensional stress
   D brittle stress

62. When two oceanic plates converge, subduction and partial melting of the mantle occurs. What type of mountains form in this scenario?

   A folded mountains
   B fault-block mountains
   C volcanic mountains
   D none of the above

63. Which of the following describes how an accretionary wedge forms at oceanic-continental plate boundaries?

   A Sediment gets scraped off of the subducting plate and gets stuck onto the continent.
   B Rivers transport and deposit sediment from the continent to the continental edge.
   C Wave action transports sediment from the ocean floor to the continental edge.
   D Volcanic material is erupted from island arcs and deposited on the continental edge.

64. Which of the following principles can be used to determine the relative ages of these rock layers shown below?

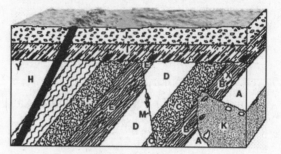

   A law of superposition
   B principle of cross-cutting relationships
   C principle of original horizontality
   D all of the above

65. What type of fossil would the footprints of a dinosaur represent?

   A preserved remains
   B a carbon film
   C a trace fossil
   D a petrified fossil

66. The principle of fossil succession makes it possible to recognize

   A a particular time period in any geographic location.
   B long periods during which deposition stopped.
   C long periods of erosion.
   D the various body parts of a fossilized organism.

GO ON

Diagnostic Test B (continued)

67. If the half-life of a particular element is 3 million years and if 1/16 of the parent material remains, how old is the material being dated?

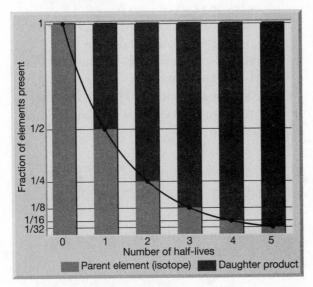

A 4 million years old
B 8 million years old
C 12 million years old
D 16 million years old

68. Which of the following is true about carbon dating?

A It is used on trees but not on fossils.
B It is very unreliable.
C Radioactivity is produced in dated samples.
D The ratio of carbon-14 to carbon-12 is compared.

69. Which of the units of the geologic time scale does the Paleozoic represent?

A an eon
B an era
C an epoch
D a period

Directions: *Use the figure below to answer Question 70.*

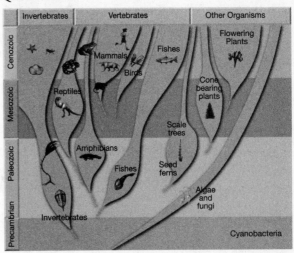

70. Which of the following organisms existed during Precambrian time?

A reptiles
B birds
C fishes
D algae

71. During the Silurian period, parts of five continents made up the vast southern landmass called

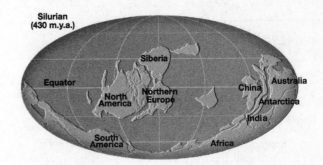

A Laurasia.
B Pangaea.
C Antarctica.
D Gondwana.

GO ON

Diagnostic Test B (continued)

72. Scientists theorize that a meteorite impact that occurred at the end of the Mesozoic era caused a mass extinction. Where did this meteorite strike Earth?

   A in Arizona
   B near Hudson Bay in northern Canada
   C in Texas
   D near the Yucatan penisula of Mexico

73. The development of angiosperms influenced the development of

   A birds and mammals.
   B reptiles and fish.
   C invertebrates.
   D gymnosperms.

74. Which of the four main ocean basins is labeled D on the map below?

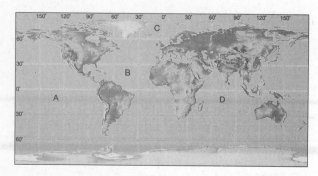

   A Indian Ocean
   B Atlantic Ocean
   C Pacific Ocean
   D Arctic Ocean

75. What forms of technology are used to measure ocean depth and features on the ocean floor?

   I. sonar
   II. satellites
   III. submersibles

   A I only
   B I and II
   C II and III
   D I, II, and III

76. Why are earthquakes common off the coast of northern California?

   A The continental shelf off the coast of California has many submarine canyons carved into it.
   B An oceanic plate is being subducted beneath a continental plate.
   C A mid-ocean ridge is forming off the California coastline.
   D Seafloor spreading is occurring at a rapid rate on California's continental margin.

77. Which of the following is **NOT** a type of ocean-floor sediment?

   A siligaseas sediment
   B biogenous sediment
   C terrigenous sediment
   D hydrogenous sediment

78. The percentage of world oil produced from offshore regions, such as the California coast has increased greatly since the 1930s. What is the main reason for this increase?

   A There is better technology for drilling platforms.
   B More oil has formed over this period of time.
   C Major reserves have been identified in more regions.
   D The amount of oil in onshore reservoirs has been greatly depleted.

79. Which of the following can be obtained by evaporating seawater?

   A halite
   B radiolarians
   C foraminifers
   D manganese nodules

GO ON

Diagnostic Test B (continued)

80. Ocean salinity is relatively constant worldwide. Which of the following can cause an increase in salinity?

   I. melting icebergs
   II. formation of sea ice
  III. surface runoff
   IV. evaporation

  A I and II
  B II and III
  C I and III
  D II and IV

81. The zone marked as Point B is the

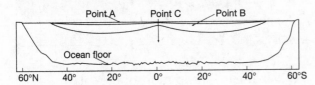

  A deep zone.
  B ocean floor.
  C mixed zone.
  D transition zone.

82. The larval stages of many marine animals, such as lobsters, crabs, and sea stars are classified as

  A phytoplankton.
  B nekton.
  C zooplankton.
  D benthos.

83. All of the following factors are used to divide the ocean into distinct marine life zones EXCEPT

  A water depth.
  B distance from shore.
  C availability of sunlight.
  D speed of currents.

Directions: *Use the diagram below to answer Question 84.*

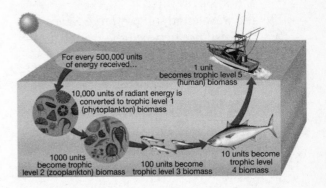

84. At each stage along this diagram, energy transfer decreases by a factor of

  A 1.
  B 10.
  C 100.
  D 1000.

85. The Gulf Stream affects the climate of Great Britain and Germany because it

  A transports heat from higher latitudes to the lower latitudes of northwest Europe.
  B transports heat from lower latitudes to the higher latitudes of northwest Europe.
  C transports heat from eastern longitudes to western longitudes.
  D transports heat from western longitudes to eastern longitudes.

86. What are density currents?

  A currents of ocean water that move horizontally across the surface
  B currents of ocean water that move vertically in the water
  C currents of ocean water set in motion by the wind
  D currents of ocean water set in motion by tides

GO ON

87. What is fetch?

   A the distance that the wind travels across open water

   B the wavelength of very large waves

   C the distance between the trough and crest of a wave

   D the area near a coast where waves begin to break

88. The gravitational attraction of the moon and sun upon Earth causes

   A ocean waves.

   B ocean currents.

   C ocean tides.

   D ocean fetches.

89. Refraction of ocean waves along a shoreline causes

   A wave action to weaken in bays.

   B wave action to increase in bays.

   C wave-cut cliffs to form.

   D tombolos to form.

90. Attempts to stabilize the shoreline in order to prevent erosion and property damage include the construction of protective structures as well as beach nourishment. These attempts result in solutions that always

   A stabilize the shoreline permanently.

   B have positive effects on the shoreline.

   C have negative effects on the shoreline.

   D interfere with some natural processes.

Directions: *Use the diagram below to answer Question 91.*

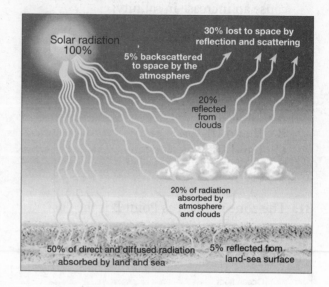

91. What happens to most of the solar radiation that reaches Earth?

   A It is lost to space by reflection and backscattering.

   B It is absorbed by clouds and gases in the atmosphere.

   C It is scattered back into space by Earth's atmosphere.

   D It is absorbed by Earth's land and water.

92. An increase in the tilt of Earth's axis with respect to the sun would

   A eliminate solar eclipses.

   B decrease the period of a year.

   C increase Earth's rotation.

   D alter seasonal changes in weather.

GO ON

Name _____ Date _____ Class _____

Diagnostic Test B (continued)

93. What are the three major mechanisms of heat transfer?

   A radiation, convection, and conduction
   B X-rays, ultraviolet radiation, and visible light
   C radiation, convection, and reflection
   D convection, conduction, and reflection

Directions: *Use the chart below to answer Question 94.*

Variation in Annual Mean Temperature Range (° C) with Latitude		
Latitude	Northern Hemisphere	Southern Hemisphere
0	0	0
15	3	4
30	13	7
45	23	6
60	30	11
75	32	26
90	40	31

94. Where is there a greater variation in mean temperature range?

   A in the Northern Hemisphere
   B in the Southern Hemisphere
   C in the winter
   D latitude 0

95. The majority of incoming solar radiation is

   A used in photosynthesis.
   B absorbed by land and water.
   C reflected from clouds.
   D absorbed by clouds and water vapor.

Directions: *Use the diagram below to answer Question 96.*

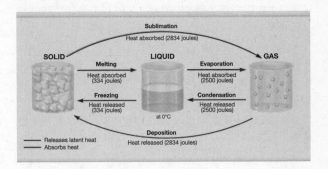

96. What changes of state does a solid go through before it changes to a gas?

   A melting and freezing
   B melting and evaporation
   C freezing and evaporation
   D freezing and condensation

97. What is relative humidity?

   A the total amount of water vapor in air at the freezing point
   B ratio of the actual water-vapor content of air compared to the amount the air can hold at that temperature
   C the total amount of water vapor that air at a particular temperature is capable of holding
   D the total amount of water vapor in the air at the boiling point of water

98. When air expands,

   A it cools.
   B it gets warmer.
   C its density increases.
   D its temperature remains constant.

GO ON

Diagnostic Test B (continued)

99. What causes a temperature inversion like the one shown in the diagram below?

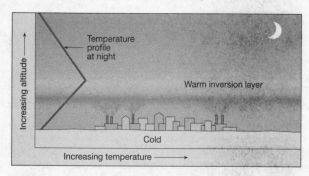

A The ground cools faster than air higher in the atmosphere on a clear night.
B The ground cools slower than air higher in the atmosphere on a foggy morning.
C The air cools faster than the ground beneath it on a cloudy night.
D The ground cools slower than the air above it on a stormy morning.

100. Which of the following clouds would be classified as a middle level cloud?

A altocumulus
B cirrus
C cirrostratus
D nimbostratus

101. Any form of water that falls from a cloud is called

A sleet.
B rain.
C precipitation.
D water vapor.

Directions: *Use the diagram below to answer Question 102.*

A Mercury Barometer

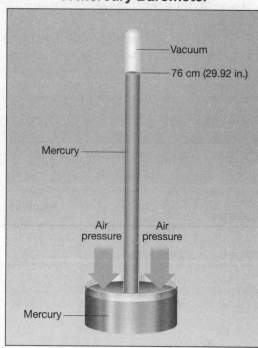

102. When air pressure increases, the mercury in the tube will

A fall.
B rise.
C evaporate.
D not change.

103. Earth's surface ocean currents and winds are deflected from their original paths as the result of

A the conveyor belt model.
B the Coriolis effect.
C plate movements.
D all of the above.

GO ON

Diagnostic Test B (continued)

104. Centers of low pressure are frequently associated with

   A sunny skies and high temperatures.
   B cloudy conditions and high temperatures.
   C sunny skies and dry weather.
   D cloudy skies and precipitation.

105. The atmosphere balances the unequal heating of Earth's surface by transporting

   A warm air toward high latitudes and cool air toward the equator.
   B cool air toward high latitudes and warm air toward the equator.
   C storms across oceans.
   D upper-level airflow in an easterly direction.

106. In what approximate direction do low pressure centers move in the United States?

   A north to south
   B south to north
   C west to east
   D east to west

107. What characteristics are used to classify air masses?

   A time of year and wind directions
   B time of year and temperature
   C similar temperatures and amounts of moisture
   D amounts of moisture and wind direction

Directions: *Use the map to help you answer Question 108.*

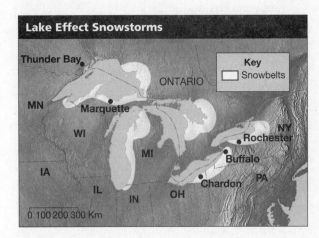

108. Which of the statement(s) are correct about lake-effect snowstorms?

   I. Lake-effect snows are localized storms.
   II. Heavy snow falls at the northern and western shores because the air absorbs large quantities of heat and moisture from the lake.
   III. The temperature of the air over the water is warmer than that of the air over land.
   IV. Heavy snow falls at the southern and eastern shores because the air absorbs large quantities of heat and moisture from the lake.

   A I and II
   B I only
   C I and III
   D I, III, and IV

GO ON

109. What type of front will form when warm air moves into an area that has been covered by cooler air?

  A cold front
  B occluded front
  C stationary front
  D warm front

110. Heavy precipitation is characteristic of which stage of a thunderstorm?

  A cumulus
  B mature
  C downdraft
  D dissipating

111. Whirling tropical cyclones with substained winds of at least 119 kilometers per hour that produce heavy rains, high winds, floods, and rough seas are known in the United States as

  A thunderstorms.
  B hurricanes.
  C tornadoes.
  D seamounts.

112. The climate of a region is determined by all of the following EXCEPT

  A longitude.
  B ocean current temperature.
  C elevation above sea level.
  D distance from the equator.

113. The leeward side of a mountain will generally be

  A cool and moist.
  B cool and dry.
  C warm and moist.
  D warm and dry.

114. Why do global winds affect climate?

  A Global winds do not affect climate in any way.
  B Global winds affect the seasons because of the Coriolis force.
  C Global winds distribute heat and moisture.
  D Global winds affect the cloud types that can form in an area.

115. The Köppen climate classification system classifies climates according to

  A elevation and latitude.
  B topography and latitude.
  C temperature and precipitation.
  D temperature and elevation.

116. The three graphs below show the temperatures and amounts of precipitation that are characteristic of humid mid-latitude climates. Note: the bars represent precipitation and the lines represent temperature. In which month does Sitka, Alaska, recieve the most precipitation?

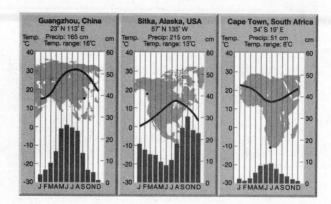

  A June
  B July
  C January
  D October

GO ON

Diagnostic Test B (continued)

117. In winter, which climate region experiences a long period during which days are very short or the sun does not rise above the horizon?

   A tropical climates
   B humid mid-latitude climates
   C polar climates
   D highland climates

118. What natural processes can change climate?

   A volcanic eruptions and plate tectonics
   B ocean circulation and solar activity
   C Earth's orbit and changes in atmospheric circulation
   D all of the above

119. What effect, if any, does the increase in CO_2 levels in the air have on global temperatures?

   A Temperatures rise.
   B Temperatures fall.
   C Temperatures fluctuate greatly.
   D There is no effect.

120. Early Greeks believed in the geocentric model of the universe, which stated that

   A the sun was the center of the universe, with planets orbiting around it.
   B the planets orbited Earth, which in turn orbited the moon.
   C Earth was the center of the universe, with the sun, the moon, and five planets orbiting around it.
   D the sun, the moon, and Earth were the only heavenly bodies in the celestial sphere.

121. What motion of Earth results in small movements of Earth's axis over a period of 26,000 years?

   A rotation
   B precession
   C revolution
   D perihelion

122. What type of eclipse is illustrated in the image below?

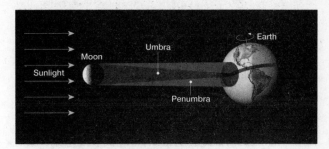

   A partial lunar eclipse
   B total lunar eclipse
   C total solar eclipse
   D partial solar eclipse

123. What is the most widely accepted model for the origin of Earth's moon?

   A The moon formed from debris that resulted from a collision between Earth and a body the size of Mars.
   B The moon was a slow-moving astroid captured by Earth's gravity and brought into a nearly circular orbit.
   C The moon formed from debris that was thrown outward shortly after the big bang.
   D The moon was a part of the planet Jupiter that escaped Jupiter's gravitational field.

GO ON

Diagnostic Test B (continued)

124. Which of the following is the best explanation of why the outer planets are so different from the inner planets?

   A Their distance from the sun resulted in their forming from gases and ices.

   B The part of the rotating cloud in which they formed was rotating faster than the center of the cloud.

   C They were too large to form from solid matter.

   D The sun's gravitational attraction on the outer planets was very strong.

125. The most prominent feature of Saturn is

   A its system of moons.

   B its system of rings.

   C the color of its atmosphere.

   D the density of its atmosphere.

126. Which of the following is **NOT** true of Pluto?

   A It has the same composition as planets far from the sun.

   B It has one moon, Charon, which orbits very close to it.

   C It is very cold and might be made of ice and rock.

   D It is considered a dwarf planet.

127. From the diagram below, where are most of the asteroids in the solar system are found?

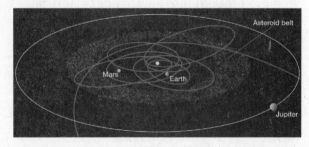

   A between the orbits of Jupiter and Saturn

   B bewteen the orbits of Earth and Mars

   C between the orbits of Mars and Jupiter

   D between the orbits of Venus and Earth

128. What is the glowing head of a comet called?

   A the coma

   B the tail

   C the nucleus

   D the nebula

129. Which of the following is **NOT** considered to be a possible source of meteoroids?

   A debris not swept up by the planets during solar system formation

   B material from the asteroid belt

   C material expelled from the sun by solar flares

   D solid remains of near-Earth comets

130. The image below shows three types of spectra. What information about stars can scientists learn from studying the absorption and emission spectra of different stars?

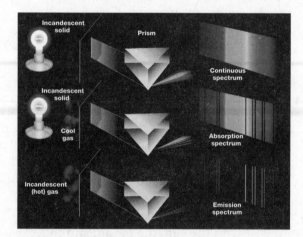

   A the size of the star

   B the star's chemical composition

   C whether planets orbit the star

   D how far away from Earth the star is

Diagnostic Test B

GO ON

Diagnostic Test B (continued)

131. How are radio telescopes used to study star life cycles?

   A They can detect cold gas clouds, which are sites of star formation.
   B They use mirrors to form images of stars in various life stages.
   C They use lenses to form images of stars in various life stages.
   D They can detect X-rays given off by black holes.

132. What types of telescopes are most commonly used to observe black holes?

   A X-ray telescopes
   B Earth-based reflecting telescopes
   C radio telescopes
   D Earth-based refracting telescopes

133. Why are space telescopes often used to study stars?

   A Radio interference prohibits the use of most optical telescopes based on Earth.
   B Their secondary mirrors do not block visible light entering the telescope.
   C The images they produce are not blurred by Earth's atmosphere.
   D Stars cannot be observed with Earth-based telescopes.

134. What are cooler, dark areas that appear in the sun's surface called?

   A solar flares
   B prominences
   C coronas
   D sunspots

Directions: *Use the diagram below to answer Question 135.*

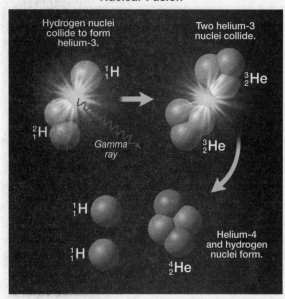

135. In the process of nuclear fusion, hydrogen nuclei combine to form a helium atom. What is the outcome of this process?

   A Hydrogen is converted to ozone.
   B Some energy is converted to matter.
   C Some matter is converted to energy.
   D Helium is converted to hydrogen.

136. Evidence indicating that planets are closer to Earth than stars includes

   A direct observations of planets passing in front of stars and parallax measurements.
   B direct observations of planets passing in front of stars and calculations of gravitational forces around black holes.
   C parallax measurements and modeling star life cycles.
   D all of the above.

GO ON

Diagnostic Test B (continued)

Directions: *Use the chart below to answer Question 137.*

Hertzsprung-Russel Diagram

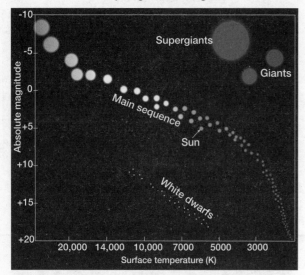

137. How does the temperature of the sun compare to the temperature range of white dwarfs?

- **A** Most white dwarfs are cooler than the sun.
- **B** Most white dwarfs are hotter than the sun.
- **C** Scientists have not determined the temperature of white dwarfs.
- **D** Like the sun, white dwarfs are main-sequence stars; thus, their temperatures fall into the same range as the sun's temperature.

138. In the diagram below, the gas pressure equals the force of gravity pushing in on the star. What type of star is shown?

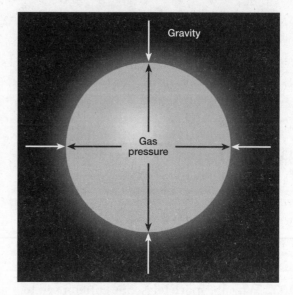

- **A** white dwarf
- **B** supergiant
- **C** black hole
- **D** main sequence star

139. What causes all stars to eventually die?

- **A** stars die when they get too hot be remain on the main sequence
- **B** stars die when they run out of fuel for nuclear fission
- **C** stars die when they run out of fuel for nuclear fusion
- **D** stars die when they become protostars

GO ON

Diagnostic Test B (continued)

140. About how wide is the Milky Way Galaxy?

  A 1 light-year
  B 100 light-years
  C 10,000 light-years
  D 100,000 light-years

141. The red shifts of distant galaxies indicate that the universe is

  A in orbit.
  B expanding.
  C collapsing.
  D contracting.

142. According to the big bang theory, the universe formed about 13.7 billion years ago and has been

  A contracting ever since.
  B contracting and expanding ever since.
  C expanding ever since.
  D getting more circular ever since.

143. What is the correct identification of the four main ocean basins shown in the diagram below?

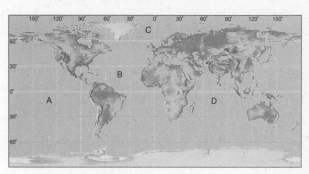

  A A: Indian, B: Arctic, C: Atlantic, D: Pacific
  B A: Atlantic, B: Pacific, C: Arctic, D: Indian
  C A: Pacific, B: Atlantic, C: Arctic, D: Indian
  D A: Arctic, B: Indian, C: Pacific, D: Atlantic

STOP

Benchmark Test 1

1. Which of the following is a subdivision of Earth science that deals with the study of the atmosphere?

   A geology
   B astronomy
   C meteorology
   D oceanography

2. What hypothesis describes how the solar system formed from a swirling cloud of dust and gases?

   A the big bang hypothesis
   B the geosphere hypothesis
   C the nebular hypothesis
   D the supernova hypothesis

3. All life on Earth is part of which of Earth's spheres?

   A the hydrosphere
   B the biosphere
   C the atmosphere
   D the geosphere

4. Earth is divided into three main layers according to their

   A age.
   B thickness.
   C composition.
   D temperature.

5. Which geological theory explains how mountains are formed and where earthquakes and volcanoes occur?

   A the nebular theory
   B the theory of plate tectonics
   C the big bang theory
   D the theory of the geosphere

Directions: *Use the globe below to answer Questions 6 and 7.*

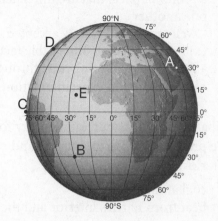

6. Which labeled point shown on the globe is located at 30 degrees north and 60 degrees east?

   A Point A
   B Point B
   C Point C
   D Point E

7. What information **CANNOT** be determined from the globe?

   A latitude and longitude of position B
   B distance in degrees of position C from position D
   C distance of position E from the prime meridian
   D elevation of position A

8. What type of map would you use to determine the difference in elevation between the top of Sugar Loaf Mountain and your campsite at the base of the mountain?

   A a geologic map
   B a mercator projection map
   C a gnomonic projection map
   D a topographic map

GO ON

9. What is a system?

   A any size group of interacting parts that make up a complex whole

   B a group of parts that are unrelated to one another

   C a well tested and widely accepted explanation for an observable fact

   D a process of gathering facts through observation and experimentation

10. What are the two sources of energy for all the processes on Earth's surface and interior?

   A coal and petroleum

   B heat from Earth's interior and the sun

   C geothermal energy and nuclear energy

   D the sun and fossil fuels

11. From which of Earth's systems could nonrenewable resources such as iron ore and copper ore be obtained?

   A from the atmosphere

   B from the biosphere

   C from the geosphere

   D from the hydrosphere

12. Which of the following is considered to be a renewable resource?

   A wheat

   B coal

   C iron ore

   D petroleum

13. The Earth-centered model of the universe was widely accepted for thousands of years. Why did this model of the universe never become a theory?

   A After it was proposed, new observations of objects in the universe proved that the idea was incorrect.

   B The model was not based on observations of objects in space.

   C The model wasn't around long enough to become a theory.

   D It was not a testable hypothesis about the universe.

14. The mineral halite has the chemical formula of $NaCl$. What forms the building blocks of this minerals and all other minerals?

   A radioactive isotopes

   B electrons

   C protons

   D atoms of elements

15. Using the diagram below, what is the atomic mass of this element?

   | 6 |
   | C |
   | Carbon |
   | 12.011 |

   A 6

   B 18

   C 12

   D 12.011

GO ON

Benchmark Test 1 (continued)

16. The unstable radioactive form of carbon, C-14 that is used to determine the age of organic material, such as the wood in ancient firepits is known as

  A an ion.
  B a proton.
  C an isotope.
  D a metal.

17. The chemical combination of two or more of the atoms of elements is called

  A a molecule.
  B a compound.
  C an isotope.
  D a mineral.

18. What type of chemical bonding forms between the sodium and chlorine atoms shown below?

  A ionic bonding
  B covalent bonding
  C metallic bonding
  D isotopic bonding

19. An earth material must meet five criteria in order to be classified as a mineral. Which of the following is **NOT** one of the criteria?

  A It must be of synthetic origin.
  B It must have a definite chemical composition.
  C It must have an orderly crystalline structure.
  D It must be a solid substance.

20. Jared ran an experiment in which he dissolved a variety of substances in a beaker filled with water. He let the beaker sit out until all of the water had evaporated and a new substance was left behind. What process of mineral formation did Jared model?

  A crystallization
  B precipitation
  C pressure and temperature
  D hydrothermal solution

21. Minerals that contain the elements silicon and oxygen are classified in what mineral group?

  A carbonates
  B sulfates
  C oxides
  D silicates

GO ON

Benchmark Test 1 (continued)

22. Which group of minerals forms structures such as chains, sheets, and three-dimensional networks?

   A halides
   B sulfates
   C carbonates
   D silicates

23. What property is the LEAST useful to use for identifying minerals?

   A hardness
   B streak
   C cleavage
   D color

24. Which index mineral is this unknown sample?

> An unknown mineral was subjected to a hardness test. It was determined that the mineral was harder than a wire nail but softer than glass.

Mohs Scale of Hardness		
Index Mineral	**Hardness**	**Common Object**
Diamond	10	
Corundum	9	
Topaz	8	
Quartz	7	
Orthoclase	6	Streak plate (6.5)
Apatite	5	Glass (5.5) Knife blade (5.1)
Fluorite	4	Wire nail (4.5)
Calcite	3	Copper penny (3.5)
Gypsum	2	Fingernail (2.5)
Talc	1	

   A quartz
   B orthoclase
   C apatite
   D fluorite

GO ON

25. A mineral that breaks unevenly to form a rough surface is said to exhibit

   A cleavage.
   B fracture.
   C hardness.
   D density.

26. You know that the density of pure gold is 19.3 grams per cubic centimeter. You have a sample which may also contain another mineral, but you can only see gold on the surface. How could you determine if the sample is pure gold or not?

   A If the density of the sample is exactly 19.3 grams per cubic centimeter it is not pure gold.
   B If the density of the sample is different from the density of pure gold, the sample contains other minerals
   C It would be impossible to determine whether the sample is pure gold or not, because all minerals have the same density.
   D Use the color and streak of the surface of the sample to determine if another mineral is present.

27. What is the tendency of a mineral to break along flat, smooth surfaces called?

   A cleavage
   B streak
   C density
   D hardness

28. Carbon dioxide enters the atmosphere through all of the following processes **EXCEPT**

   A respiration.
   B photosynthesis.
   C burning of biomass.
   D weathering of carbonate rock.

29. What is a naturally-occurring solid mixture of one or more minerals?

   A a fossil
   B a rock
   C an isotope
   D an element

30. What type of rock forms from cooling magma?

   A igneous
   B metamorphic
   C sedimentary
   D sediments

31. The diagram shows a model of the rock cycle. What type of rock is formed deep inside Earth under conditions of high temperature and pressure?

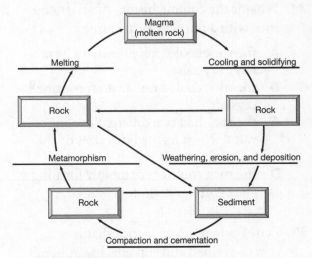

   A igneous rock
   B metamorphic rock
   C sediments
   D sedimentary rock

GO ON

Benchmark Test 1 (continued)

32. In the rock cycle, which of the following processes are driven by energy from the sun?

  A weathering of rocks to form sediment
  B formation of magma deep within Earth
  C formation of metamorphic rocks deep beneath the surface
  D crystallization of igneous rock in batholliths

33. What is true of extrusive igneous rocks?

  A They form from cooling lava.
  B They form deep beneath Earth's surface.
  C They form when magma hardens beneath Earth's surface.
  D They can have large mineral crystals, because they cool very slowly.

34. What is the cooling history of an igneous rock with a porphyritic texture?

  A the rock cooled very slowly to form large crystals
  B the rock cooled rapidly to form small crystals
  C the rock had two different cooling rates, which formed two sizes of mineral crystals
  D the rock cooled very rapidly forming a glass with no definite crystals

35. Zane finds an igneous rock that is coarse-grained and contains the minerals quartz, potassium feldspar, biotite, and sodium-rich plagioclase feldspar. How should Zane classify this rock?

  A as rhyolite
  B as diorite
  C as gabbro
  D as granite

36. What happens when a stream that is transporting large sediment grains slows down and loses energy?

  A the large grains will continue to be transported by the stream
  B the large grains will be deposited
  C the stream will be able to erode more of its banks
  D the large grains will become cemented in the stream bed

37. A layer of sedimentary rock is exposed in a road cut. The rock is made up of rounded grains that are over 2 millimeters in diameter. How would you classify this type of rock?

  A as the clastic sedimentary rock siltstone
  B as the chemical sedimentary rock sandstone
  C as the clastic sedimentary rock conglomerate
  D as the clastic sedimentary rock breccia

38. Which of the following features are normally found only in sedimentary rocks?

  A fossils
  B the mineral quartz
  C a coarse-grained texture
  D different sizes of mineral grains

39. Why could the area surrounding an igneous body that formed from cooling magma be a likely location to find rock that has undergone metamorphism?

  A increased pressure on the surrounding rock causes regional metamorphism
  B heat and hydrothermal fluids from the magma causes contact metamorphism
  C the magma causes the surrounding rock to become folded resulting in regional metamorphism
  D heat from the magma does not reach the surrounding rocks, so no metamorphism can occur

GO ON

Benchmark Test 1 (continued)

40. Regional metamorphism that occurs during mountain building is characterized by

   A low-grade metamorphism and local deformation.

   B low-grade metamorphism and large-scale deformation.

   C high-grade metamorhism and local deformation.

   D high-grade metamorphism and large-scale deformation.

41. Which of the major agents of metamorphism is responsible for the deformation of the rock layers in the image below?

   A increased heat only

   B hydrothermal fluids

   C increased pressure

   D increased erosion rates

42. Which of the following is NOT classified as a foliated metamorphic rock?

   A gneiss

   B marble

   C schist

   D slate

43. On a field trip, Evan found a metamorphic rock which has thick bands of different minerals. The main minerals are coarse grains of quartz and feldspar. How should Evan classify this rock?

   A as gneiss

   B as marble

   C as schist

   D as quartzite

44. Which of following is an example of a nonrenewable resource?

   A iron ore used to make steel

   B corn used to make an additive to gasoline

   C wheat used to make bread

   D cotton used to make clothing

45. The diagram below shows a well drilled for what type of resources?

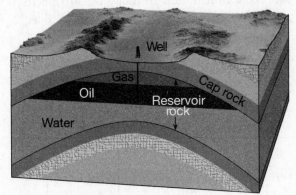

   A renewable resources

   B fossil fuels

   C nonmetallic minerals

   D tar sands and oil shale

GO ON

Benchmark Test 1 (continued)

46. An estimated 35 billion barrels of oil may be produced from the mining of deposits located in the Canadian province of Alberta. These reserves may help replace decreasing supplies of petroleum. What type of deposits are these reserves?

    A coal
    B uranium ore
    C tar sands
    D hydrothermal copper deposits

47. In the areas around magma chambers, hot, metal-rich fluids can form deposits of valuable minerals in fractures. What are these types of mineral deposits called?

    A placer deposits
    B hydrothermal vein deposits
    C layered igneous deposits
    D regional metamorphic deposits

48. What nonmetallic mineral resource is used to manufacture everyday items, such as lubricants, pencil leads, and high-tech fishing tackle?

    A halite
    B gypsum
    C graphite
    D sulfur

49. Which of the following are two advantages of solar energy.

    A It is a free fuel and is non-polluting.
    B It is non-polluting and the equipment is very inexpensive.
    C It can be used on cloudy days and it non-polluting.
    D It can be converted to electricity more easily than other sources of energy.

50. What reaction is used in nuclear power plants to generate energy?

    A nuclear fission
    B natural radioactive decay
    C nuclear fusion
    D crystalization of uranium

51. What alternative energy source is illustrated in the image below?

    A nuclear energy
    B geothermal energy
    C hydroelectric power
    D wind energy

52. In 1966 a dam was constructed across the mouth of the Rance River in France. Flow of water into and out of the river drives turbines and generates electricity. What alternative energy source does this dam represent?

    A wind energy
    B geothermal energy
    C tidal power
    D hydrothermal power

GO ON

Benchmark Test 1 (continued)

53. Which of the following is an example of a nonpoint source of pollution of freshwater resources?

A leaking septic tank
B outflow pipe from a chemical plant
C leak from an underground gasoline storage tank
D oil and salt from highways and roads

54. Why is the greenhouse effect produced by carbon dioxide, methane, and water vapor in the atmosphere important to life on Earth?

A They cause air pollution and breathing problems.
B They keep Earth warm enough for life.
C They protect organisms from harmful ultaviolet radiation.
D They are important in the process of respiration in animals.

55. Which of following is **NOT** an example of a land resource?

A forests
B soil
C copper
D freshwater

56. What environmental law passed by the U.S. Congress required toxic or hazardous substances to be stored, transported, and disposed of under strict guidelines?

A 1972 Clean Water Act
B 1974 Safe Drinking Water Act
C 1970 Clean Air Act
D 1976 Resource Conservation and Recovery Act

57. The Clean Air Act established National Ambient Air Quality Standards for all the following pollutants **EXCEPT**

A water vapor.
B carbon monoxide.
C sulfur dioxide.
D ozone.

58. What is Integrated Pest Management?

A using compost to add organic material to the soil, reducing the need for fertilizer
B using natural predators or vacumming pests off leaves to reduce the number of pests
C using a combination of artifical fertilizers and pesticides to increase crop yields
D use contour plowing and strip cropping to present soil erosion

59. The domes known as Liberty Cap and Half Dome in Yosemite National Park formed mostly as the result of

A chemical weathering by water.
B exfoliation.
C biological agents acting on the granite.
D spheroidal weathering of the granite.

60. How does water contribute to chemical weathering?

A It freezes and thaws many times to cause frost wedging.
B It absorbs gases from the air and ground that react with minerals.
C It causes burrowing animals to bring rocks to the surface where weathering is more rapid.
D It causes large masses of rock to be exposed and eroded, causing exfoliation.

GO ON

Benchmark Test 1 (continued)

61. Which of the blocks in the diagram below would undergo the most chemical weathering?

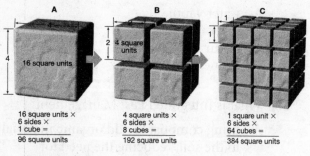

16 square units ×
6 sides ×
1 cube =
96 square units

4 square units ×
6 sides ×
8 cubes =
192 square units

1 square unit ×
6 sides ×
64 cubes =
384 square units

 A block A
 B block B
 C block C
 D all blocks would undergo the same amount of chemical weathering

62. Which of the following is **NOT** a factor in soil development?

 A parent material
 B wind direction
 C slope
 D climate

63. Which of the soil horizons would contain the lowest amount of organic material?

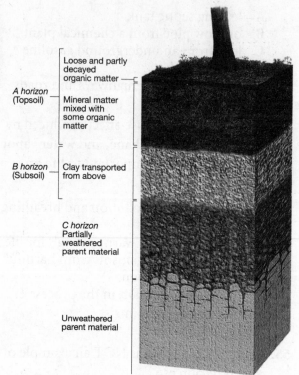

 A A horizon
 B B horizon
 C C horizon
 D All horizons contain the same amount of organic material.

64. Which type of soil is commonly found in temperate areas that receive more than 63 cm of rain per year, such as forested areas of the eastern United States?

 A humus
 B laterite
 C pedalfer
 D pedocal

Benchmark Test 1

GO ON

65. Which activity or event would probably cause the **LEAST** soil erosion?

   A clear-cut logging a forest on a steep slope

   B plowing along the contours of hills and planting corn

   C clearing all the plants from an area to build a shopping mall

   D a forest fire that destroyed all the vegetation in an area of steep hills

66. What is a mass movement?

   A movement of rock and soil downslope under the influence of gravity

   B movement of water in a channel under the influence of gravity

   C movement of wind over an area that has been cleared of vegetation

   D movement of soil and rock in a stream or river channel

67. Which of the following would **NOT** be the cause of a mass movement on a slope?

   A earthquake near the area

   B unusually heavy rainfall in the area

   C forest fire destroying the vegetation on the slope

   D high winds in the area

68. How would the mass movement shown in the diagram below be classified?

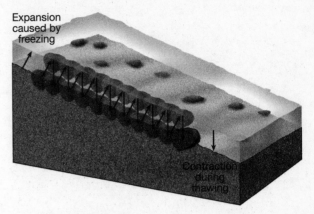

   A as a mudflow

   B as a rockslide

   C as creep

   D as a rockfall

STOP

Name _____ Date _____ Class _____

Benchmark Test 2

Directions: *Use the diagram below to answer Questions 1 and 2.*

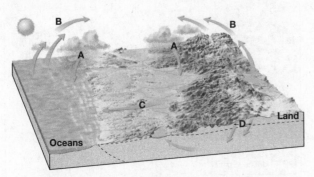

1. What process do the arrows labeled B in the diagram illustrate?

  A infiltration
  B precipitation
  C evaporation
  D runoff

2. The diagram shows the water cycle. Earth's water cycle is said to be in balance. What is in balance within Earth's water cycle?

  A amount of infiltration is balanced by average annual precipitation
  B average annual precipitation is balanced by amount of evaporation
  C amount of evaporation is balanced by the amount of runoff
  D amount of runoff is balanced by the amount of condesation

3. What is the major factor that determines the ability of a stream to erode and transport material?

  A the depth of the stream
  B the age of the stream
  C how straight or curved the channel is
  D the velocity of water in the stream

Directions: *Use the chart below to answer Question 4.*

Some of the World's Largest Rivers		
River	**Country**	**Average Discharge m³/s**
Ganges	India	18,700
Amazon	Brazil	212,400
Paran	Argentina	14,900
Lena	Russia	15,500
Congo	Zaire	39,650
Orinoco	Venezuela	17,000
Yangtze	China	21,800
Mississippi	United States	17,300
Brahmaputra	Bangladesh	19,800
Yenisei	Russia	17,400

4. Which river shown has the lowest average discharge?

  A Yangtze
  B Lena
  C Amazon
  D Paran

5. What is the base level of a stream?

  A the highest point to which a stream can erode its channel
  B the lowest point to which a stream can erode its channel
  C the lowest point at which a tributary enters a stream
  D the highest level to which a stream can build its floodplain

GO ON

Benchmark Test 2 (continued)

6. What are the three main ways that streams erode their channels?

    A by abrasion, dissolving soluble material, and deflation
    B by abrasion, grinding, and dissolving soluble material
    C by grinding, flooding, and deposition
    D by deposition, weathering, and infiltration

7. An accumulation of sediment that is formed where a stream enters a lake or an ocean is called

    A a levee.
    B an alluvial fan.
    C a meander.
    D a delta.

8. A cross-section of the Yellowstone River valley would show that the valley has a distinct V-shape. What agent of erosion carved this valley?

    A mass movements
    B running water
    C wind
    D glaciers

9. Which of the following is NOT a common method used to control flooding?

    A building flood control dams
    B building artificial levees
    C diverting water from one river to another
    D limiting development on floodplains

10. The map shows the Mississippi River drainage basin. What is a drainage basin?

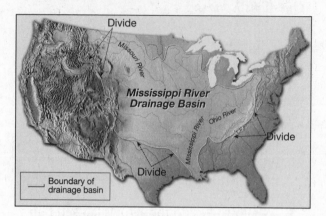

    A the land area that contributes water to a stream
    B the land area where people use the river as the sole water source
    C the land area where all streams flow to the south
    D the area that is threatened from flooding by the stream

11. Permeable rock layers or sediments that transmit groundwater are

    A geysers.
    B springs.
    C aquifers.
    D drainage basins.

GO ON

Benchmark Test 2 (continued)

12. What is the source for the hotter than normal water in most hot springs?

  A heat from the sun
  B heat from cooling igneous rock
  C heat from the friction of water movement
  D heat from burning of fossil fuels

13. The diagrams show the level of the water table in an area before and after heavy pumping of groundwater. How does the large amount of groundwater being pumped threaten the groundwater supplies for other wells in the area?

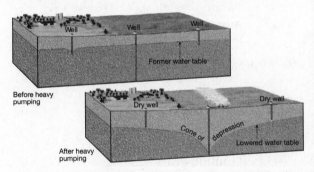

  A other wells in the area are not affected by the heavy pumping
  B the water table has been raised to a higher level in the area
  C the other wells in the area will have higher rates of groundwater flow
  D other wells in the area may go dry as the level of the water table drops

14. What is a dripstone feature that hangs down from a cavern's ceiling called?

  A stalagmite
  B stalactite
  C calcite
  D soda straw column

15. What feature commonly found in areas with karst topography is shown in the image below?

  A a cavern
  B a stalactite
  C an aquifer
  D a sinkhole

GO ON

Benchmark Test 2 (continued)

16. What type of glaciers are shown in the diagrams below?

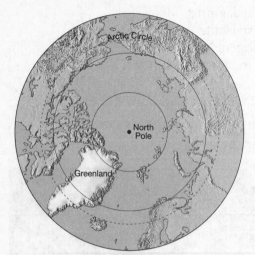

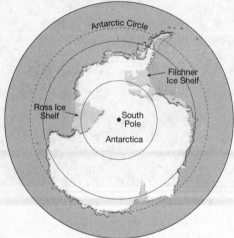

A valley glaciers
B ice sheets
C mountain glaciers
D ice moraines

17. Which of the following statements does **NOT** describe glacial flow?

A caused by either basal slip or plastic flow
B happens at various rates of speed
C only occurs in valley glaciers
D refers to the movement of glaciers

18. What landscape feature is formed when a glacier erodes a bowl-shaped depression surrounded by steep rock walls on three sides at the head of a valley?

A a cirque
B a horn
C an arete
D a moraine

19. Approximately when did the most recent ice age begin?

A 10,000 years ago
B 2 to 3 million years ago
C 30,000 years ago
D 20 million years ago

20. What type of streams are most common in desert areas?

A large rivers that flow all year long
B ephemeral streams that carry water away from salt lakes
C ephemeral streams that only carry water after rains
D permanent streams that flow at all times

GO ON

Benchmark Test 2 (continued)

21. Why is mechanical weathering the main form of weathering in most deserts?

   A All the weathering in deserts is chemical weathering.

   B There is no water at all in deserts.

   C There are no plants at all in deserts.

   D Deserts have less moisture and fewer plants than non-desert areas.

22. A rocky surface layer known as desert pavement is caused by what process?

   A deflation

   B abrasion

   C chemical weathering

   D dissolving of soluble material

23. What is the desert landform shown in the images below?

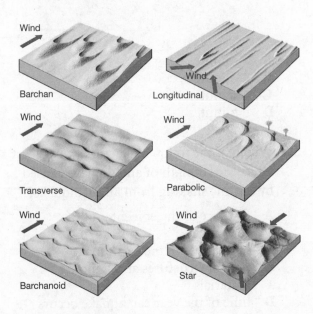

   A loess deposit

   B moraine

   C sand dune

   D desert pavement

24. Which of the following does **NOT** affect the type of dune that forms in a desert?

   A amount of vegetation

   B amount of rainfall

   C wind speed

   D amount of sand available

25. What is the area on Earth's surface directly above where an earthquake starts called?

   A the fault

   B the epicenter

   C the focus

   D the eye

26. Earthquakes occur when

   A any movement along a fault takes place.

   B an epicenter forms.

   C deformed rock snaps back into place along a fault.

   D liquefaction takes place.

27. A smaller earthquake that occurs several days before a major earthquake is known as

   A a foreshock.

   B a surface quake.

   C a tsunamis.

   D an aftershock.

GO ON

28. What type of seismic wave is shown in the diagram?

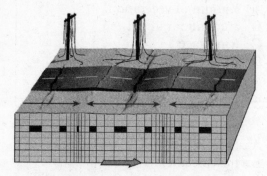

   A surface wave
   B P wave
   C S wave
   D transverse wave

29. Earthquake intensity, as measured on the Modified Mercalli scale, is based on

   A the amount of damage done by an earthquake.
   B the amplitude of an earthquake's seismic waves.
   C the moment magnitude value of an earthquake.
   D the wavelength of the largest seismic waves.

30. Which of the following factors is **NOT** considered when computing an earthquake's moment magnitude?

   A distance to the epicenter
   B rigidity of the broken rock
   C surface area of the fault involved
   D area of the surface break

31. Use the graph to determine what the difference in arrival times of the P waves and S waves would be for an earthquake that is 1000 kilometers from this seismic station.

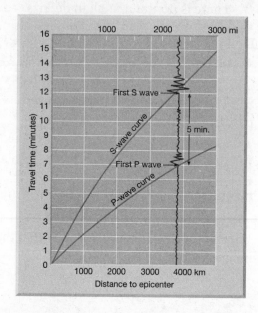

   A 1 minute
   B 2 minutes
   C 4 minutes
   D 5 minutes

32. Which of the following factors would **least** affect the strength of and damage caused by seismic shaking from an earthquake?

   A distance to the epicenter of the earthquake
   B magnitude of the earthquake
   C type of structures and building materials
   D time of the year earthquake occurs

GO ON

Benchmark Test 2 (continued)

33. Which of the following would reduce the damage to buildings caused by a major earthquake?

   A installing new gas lines without automatic shut-off values

   B building unreinforced walls in wood-frame houses

   C construction of tall nonreinforced brick buildings

   D construction of tall buildings with base-isolators

34. Which of the layers of Earth's interior shown in the diagram forms a thin, rocky layer divided into oceanic and continental types?

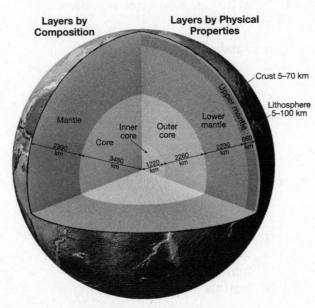

   A the crust

   B the mantle

   C the outer core

   D the inner core

35. What does the inner core of Earth consist of?

   A liquid layer of iron-nickel alloy

   B layer of the rock peridotite

   C solid layer of iron-nickel alloy

   D layer of granite

36. What information did scientists obtain about Earth's interior from the study of the paths of the P-waves and S-waves from earthquakes?

   A age of Earth

   B identification of the boundaries between Earth's layers

   C determined that the outer core was solid

   D determined that the inner core was liquid

37. What evidence did Alfred Wegener **NOT** use in his proposed continental drift hypothesis?

   A fit of coastlines of Africa and South America

   B matching fossils found on different continents

   C ancient climate changes

   D paleomagnetic data from the ocean floors

GO ON

Name _____ Date _____ Class _____

Benchmark Test 2 (continued)

38. How do the mountain ranges shown in the map below support the hypothesis of continental drift?

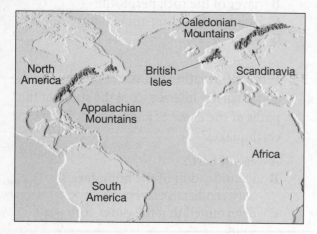

A The mountain ranges are different ages and contain different structures.
B The mountain ranges are similar in age and have similar structures and rock types.
C The mountain ranges contain completely different types of rocks.
D The mountain ranges do not provide evidence of continental drift.

39. Wegener's hypothesis of continental drift was rejected because

A he was not considered a serious scientist.
B he did not use accurate geological data.
C his climate, rock data, fossil data, and structural data was incorrect.
D he could not provide a reasonable mechanism for continental movement.

40. Which of the labeled features in the diagram represents a mid-ocean ridge?

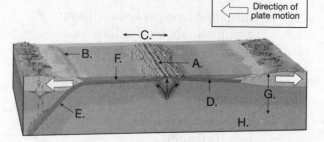

A feature C
B feature E
C feature B
D feature D

41. What process forms new oceanic lithosphere?

A subduction
B volcanic eruptions along mid-ocean ridges
C volcanic eruptions in ocean trenches
D earthquakes in rift zones

42. Earthquake patterns show that there is a link between which of the following?

A ocean drilling and earthquake frequency
B ocean ridges and ancient climates
C deep-focus earthquakes and ocean trenches
D weather and seismic activity

43. What theory states that Earth's lithospheric plates move slowly relative to one another driven by convection currents in the mantle?

A plate evolution
B uniformitarianism
C plate tectonics
D paleomagnetism

GO ON

Benchmark Test 2 (continued)

44. What do the boundaries between tectonic plates consist of?

   A deep faults
   B the edges of continents
   C the shorelines of the ocean basins
   D areas of no deformation

Directions: *Use the diagram below to answer Question 45.*

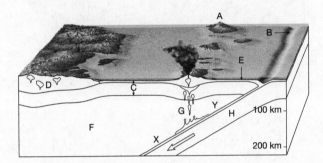

45. The type of plate boundary illustrated in the diagram is

   A a divergent plate boundary.
   B an oceanic-oceanic convergent plate boundary.
   C an oceanic-continental convergent plate boundary.
   D a transform fault boundary.

46. What is the driving force for plate movement?

   A continental rifts
   B paleomagnetism
   C fossil relocation
   D thermal convection

47. What process involves old ocean lithosphere being pulled by gravity deep into the mantle?

   A rising mantle plumes
   B formation of hot spots
   C ridge-push
   D slab-pull

48. What effect does water content have on the melting point of rock deep within Earth if the pressure is held constant?

   A water content has no effect on the melting point of rock
   B an increased water content will decrease the melting point of rock
   C an increased water content will increase the melting point of rock
   D decreased water content will decrease the melting point of rock

49. Where would a volcanic island arc form?

   A along a divergent boundary
   B along an oceanic-continental plate boundary
   C along an oceanic-oceanic plate boundary
   D along a continental-continental plate boundary

50. What type of eruption could be expected from a volcano with granitic magma with a high viscosity and gas content?

   A very quiet eruption
   B moderate eruption
   C explosive eruption
   D quiet eruption

51. What is the cooler, slower-moving basaltic lava called?

   A pahoehoe lava
   B aa lava
   C lapilli lava
   D cinder lava

GO ON

52. The type of volcano shown in the diagram below is

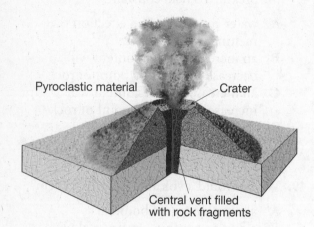

Pyroclastic material   Crater

Central vent filled
with rock fragments

  A   a shield volcano made of lava flows.
  B   a composite cone, which erupts quietly.
  C   a cinder cone, which erupts violently.
  D   a hot spot volcano, which erupts basaltic lava.

53. How does a volcanic neck form?

  A   when erosion exposes the hardened magma in a volcano's pipe
  B   by repeated eruptions of very fluid basaltic lava from a fissure
  C   when an empty magma chamber collapses
  D   when an oceanic plate moves over a rising mantle plume

54. Which of the intrusive igneous features shown in the diagram below are formed when magma moves into fractures that cut across rock layers?

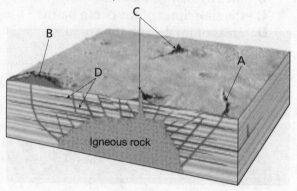

Igneous rock

  A   dikes
  B   laccoliths
  C   volcanic necks
  D   sills

55. What intrusive igneous feature is similar to a batholith but has a surface exposure of less than 100 square kilometers?

  A   a dike
  B   a sill
  C   a stock
  D   a laccolith

STOP

Benchmark Test 3

1. What factors affect the deformation of rock?

   A age of rock, temperature, pressure, and time
   B age of rock, type of rock, temperature, and time
   C type of rock, temperature, pressure, and time
   D type of rock, size of rock, age of rock, and time

2. Which of the following produces a change in the size and shape of a rock without breaking it?

   A ductile deformation
   B brittle failure
   C fracture
   D brittle deformation

3. Which of the following mountain ranges would have the thickest crust?

   A old mountain range with average height of 1000 meters above sea level
   B young mountain range with average height of 4500 meters above sea level
   C old mountain range with average height of 1800 meters above sea level
   D young mountain range with average height of 6000 meters above sea level

4. Large downfolds of rock layers are called

   A monoclines.
   B synclines.
   C anticlines.
   D horsts.

5. Strike-slip faults, like the faults in the San Andreas Fault system, are usually a result of

   A shear stress.
   B tensional stress.
   C compressional stress.
   D strike-slip stress.

6. What type of mountains are shown in the diagram?

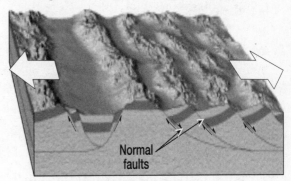

Normal faults

   A folded mountains
   B fault-block mountains
   C dome mountains
   D volcanic mountains

GO ON

7. Domes are large, roughly circular structures formed by the upwarping of rock layers. What pattern based on the age of the sedimentary rock layers would you observe in a dome?

   A Rock layers would form a circular pattern with the rock ages the same everywhere.

   B Rock layers would form a circular pattern with the youngest rocks in the center and older rocks along the edges.

   C Rock layers would form a circular pattern with the oldest rocks in the center and the youngest rocks along the edges.

   D Rock layers would form a pattern of parallel ridges with the youngest rocks in the center and the oldest rocks along the edges.

8. Mountains at a continental-continental margin form when

   A lava is added to the mountain range's height.

   B the oceanic crust pushes the continental crust higher.

   C neither plate gets subducted and continental crust gets pushed upward.

   D the nearby oceanic crust sinks lower.

9. What type of mountains are the mid-ocean ridges?

   A folded mountains
   B fault-block mountains
   C dome mountains
   D volcanic mountains

10. What is continental accretion?

   A when fragments of crust collide with a continental plate and become stuck to the continent

   B when fragments of crust are rifted away from a large continental block and become separate continents

   C when sequences of rock are deformed into large upfolded structures

   D when sequences of rock are deformed into large downfolded structures

11. What three major idea do geologists use when they study Earth history?

   A Earth is very young, uniformitarianism, and evidence of past geologic events and life forms is preserved in the rock record

   B Earth is very old, processes operating today have never occurred before, evidence of past geologic events and life forms is preserved in the rock record

   C Earth is very old, uniformitarianism, rock record preserves few past geologic events and life forms

   D Earth is very old, uniformitarianism, evidence of past geologic events and life forms is preserved in the rock record

GO ON

Benchmark Test 3 (continued)

12. Use the image below to determine which feature is the oldest; Fault B, Dike B, the batholith, or the sill?

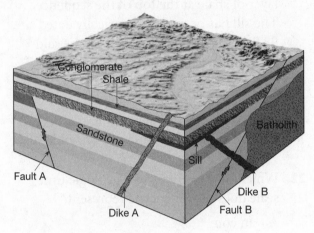

A Fault B is oldest.
B Dike B is oldest.
C Batholith is oldest.
D Sill is oldest.

13. Which of the labeled surfaces shown in the diagram is an angular unconformity?

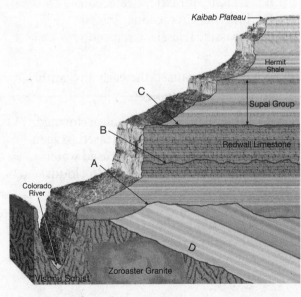

A surface A
B surface B
C surface C
D surface D

14. What type of fossil would an insect preserved in amber represent?

A preserved remains
B a carbon film
C a trace fossil
D a petrified fossil

15. Which of the following situations is most likely to produce a fossil?

A An earthworm dies while underground.
B A fish dies in the ocean and is covered by sand.
C A squirrel dies under a tree.
D A fly dies in midair.

16. The principle of fossil succession states that

A life forms have changed over time due to natural selection.
B fossils are randomly distributed through rock layers.
C fossils cannot be used to recognize the rocks of a particular time period.
D fossil organisms succeed one another in a definite and determinable order.

17. A sedimentary rock unit contained fossils from corals, sea fans, and fish. What type of ancient environment does this rock unit MOST likely represent?

A prairie-like land environment
B shallow tropical ocean environment
C cold, polar land environment
D deep-ocean environment

GO ON

Benchmark Test 3 (continued)

18. According to the chart below, one-quarter of the radioactive parent remains after

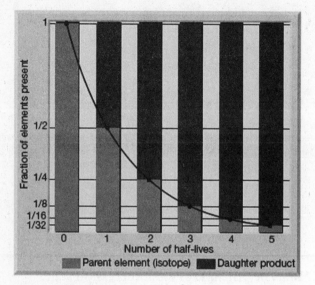

A one half-life.
B two half-lives.
C four half-lives.
D three half-lives.

19. A sample of basalt is dated using the ratio of the radioactive isotopes potassium-40/ argon-40. The half-life of potassium-40 is 1.3 billion years. If one-sixteenth of the parent potassium-40 remains in the sample, how old is the basalt sample?

A 1.3 billion years old
B 2.6 billion years old
C 3.9 billion years old
D 5.2 billion years old

20. Which of the following could be radiometrically dated using carbon-14?

A sample of granite
B deer bone found in a Native American fire pit
C fossil clam found in a Devonian limestone unit
D moon rock

21. A sequence of rock layers consists of a layer of sandstone at the base, followed by a layer of limestone, a volcanic sill, and a layer of shale at the top of the sequence. The sill has been radiometrically dated as 98 million years old. Which can be said about the age of the shale layer?

A It is older than 98 million years old.
B It is exactly 98 million years old.
C It is younger than 98 million years old.
D It is at least 200 million years old.

22. Which of the units of the geologic time scale does the Oligocene represent?

A an eon
B an era
C an epoch
D a period

23. Which of the following list the periods of the Mesozoic Era from oldest to youngest.

A Cretaceous, Triassic, Jurassic
B Triassic, Jurassic, Cretaceous
C Jurassic, Cretaceous, Triassic
D Jurassic, Triassic, Cretaceous

24. What events caused the early Precambrian atmosphere to change?

A Organisms evolved that performed photosynthesis and released oxygen.
B Volcanic eruptions released water vapor that condensed into clouds.
C As Earth's surface cooled, water evaporated, releasing water vapor and oxygen into the atmosphere.
D Torrential rains filled the ocean basins with water that evaporated, releasing oxygen into the atmosphere.

GO ON

Benchmark Test 3 (continued)

Directions: *Use the diagram below to answer Question 25.*

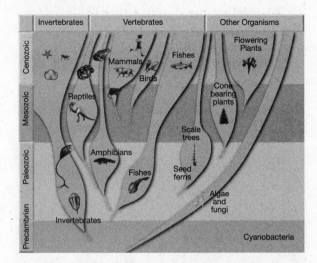

25. Which of the following organisms evolved by the late Precambrian?

   A reptiles and dinosaurs
   B flightless birds
   C flowering plants
   D multicellular invertebrates

26. How did early Earth differ from Earth today?

   A Early Earth was molten and had no oxygen in its atmosphere.
   B Early Earth had three distinct layers but had no oxygen in its atmosphere.
   C Early Earth was molten and had abundant oxygen in its atmosphere.
   D Early Earth had three distinct layers and had abundant oxygen in its atmosphere.

27. What major physical feature developed during early Paleozoic time and improved the survival of Earth's early organisms?

   A better vision in both light and dark conditions
   B ability to change directions quickly to escape predators
   C development of hard parts such as shells and bones
   D more complex body systems

28. What major group first appears in the Mesozoic Era?

   A mammals
   B reptiles
   C amphibians
   D land plants

29. The impact of a large meteorite at the end of the Cretaceous period resulted in what major geologic event?

   A the formation of the Rocky Mountains
   B the opening of the present-day Atlantic Ocean
   C a major mass extinction
   D a major period of volcanic eruptions

30. What adaptations allowed mammals to become widespread and successful during the Cenozoic Era?

   A cold-blooded metabolism and ability to fly
   B warm-blooded metabolism, more efficient heart and lungs
   C amniotic egg, cold-blooded metabolism
   D laying eggs in water, first lungs for breathing oxygen

GO ON

Benchmark Test 3 (continued)

31. Which of the following major geologic events occurred in the Cenozoic Era?

A formation of the supercontinent Rodinia

B breakup of Pangaea

C oxygen first present in the atmosphere

D major period of continental glaciation

32. Why is Earth often called the blue planet?

A the color of the atmosphere is blue

B over 70 percent of the planet is covered by water

C over 70 percent of the planet is covered by land

D about 30 percent of Earth is covered by water

33. Which of the four main ocean basins is labeled A on the map below?

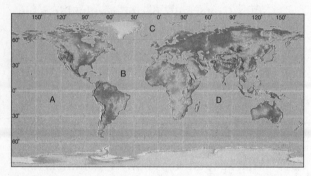

A Indian Ocean

B Atlantic Ocean

C Pacific Ocean

D Arctic Ocean

34. What is bathymetry?

A measurement of the chemistry of ocean water

B measurement of the ocean depth and topography of the ocean floor

C measurement of the height of mountains on land

D measurement of currents in the oceans

35. What technology used to study the ocean floor is shown in the image below?

A satellites used to measure sea-surface height

B submersibles to study the deep-sea

C sonar to measure the depth to the ocean floor

D radar to measure sea-surface height

36. Point C on the diagram below refers to the

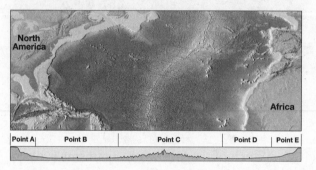

A mid-ocean ridge.

B ocean basin floor.

C deep-ocean trench.

D continental margin.

37. Which of the following describes the area of the continental margin known as the continental slope?

A gently sloping submerged surface that extends from the shoreline

B steep area that marks the boundary between continental crust and ocean crust

C a gradual incline that may be up to hundreds of meters wide

D extremely flat area with thick sediment accumulation

GO ON

Benchmark Test 3 (continued)

38. Which statement BEST describes the extent of the mid-ocean ridge?

  A It runs down the middle of the Atlantic Ocean.
  B It encircles the Pacific Ocean basin.
  C It connects the Pacific Ocean to the Arctic Ocean and the Indian Ocean.
  D It runs through all of the world's oceans.

39. What type of seafloor sediment is consists mainly of mineral grains eroded from rocks on land?

  A calcareous ooze
  B siliceous ooze
  C hydrogenous sediment
  D terrigenous sediment

40. Which ocean floor sediment has its source on land?

  A manganese nodules
  B salts
  C sand
  D calcium carbonate

41. Which of the following locations has NOT been identified as having major offshore oil reserves?

  A Chesapeake Bay
  B Gulf of Mexico
  C North Sea
  D Southern California Coast

42. Gas hydrates found in deep-ocean sediments might be viable energy resources in the future because

  A gas hydrates are plentiful and would reduce the dependence on oil and coal.
  B gas hydrates do not break down at surface temperatures and pressures.
  C gas hydrates occur only beneath the deep ocean floor.
  D gas hydrates contain petroleum, which is mixed with mud.

43. What is a potential source of metals from the ocean?

  A manganese nodules
  B gas hydrate deposits
  C sand and gravel deposits
  D evaporative salts in sea water

44. On the graph, in what units is salinity expressed?

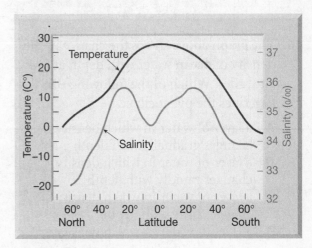

  A in percent
  B in parts per hundred
  C in parts per thousand
  D in degrees celsius

GO ON

45. What are the two main sources of salt in ocean water?
    A melting of icebergs and chemical weathering of rocks on land
    B chemical and mechanical weathering of rocks on land
    C chemical weathering of rocks on land and volcanic eruptions
    D volcanic eruptions and melting of icebergs

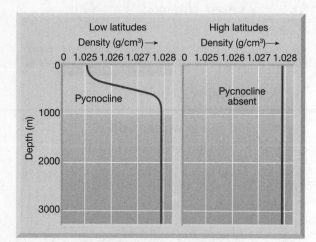

46. The graph above shows the change in the density of ocean water with depth at low lattitudes. Which of the following BEST describes the pycnocline?

    A a layer of water in which density changes gradually with depth
    B a layer of water in which density changes rapidly with depth
    C a layer of water in which density changes little with depth
    D a layer of water in which density is constant with depth

47. Oceanographers generally recognize three vertical zones in most parts of the open ocean: a shallow surface mixed zone, a transition zone, and a deep zone. What property is used to differentiate these zones?

    A water density
    B light penetration
    C circulation patterns
    D marine life forms

48. How would a crinoid that lives attached to a coral reef in a shallow tropical ocean be classified?

    A benthos
    B zooplankton
    C phytoplankton
    D nekton

49. A shark, a tuna, and a squid would be classified as

    A phytoplankton.
    B nekton.
    C zooplankton.
    D benthos.

50. Where do most benthic organisms live?

    A on the abyssal plains
    B in shallow coastal areas in the photic zone
    C in deep ocean water in the aphotic zone
    D in shallow water in the aphotic zone

51. In the photic zone,

    A hydrothermal vents support communities of organisms.
    B phytoplankton use sunlight to produce food.
    C there is no sunlight.
    D seasonal changes do not affect organisms.

GO ON

Benchmark Test 3 (continued)

52. According to the graph below, in what month are zooplankton most abundant?

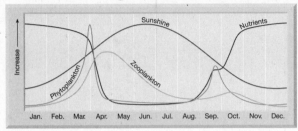

A January
B April
C August
D December

Directions: *Use the diagram below to answer Question 53.*

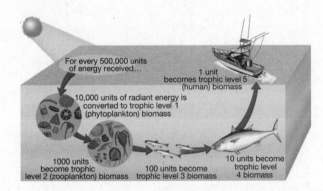

53. What percentage of the energy received by phytoplankton is converted to food, which is then available at the next tropic level?

A 10 percent
B 50 percent
C 100 percent
D 2 percent

54. What advantage do organisms that feed in a food web have that organisms that feed in a food chain do not have?

I. greater variety
II. less chance of running out of food
III. protection from predators

A I only
B I and II
C I, II, and III
D II and III

Directions: *Use the diagram below to answer Question 55.*

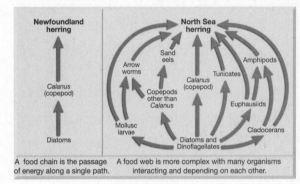

55. Newfoundland herring eat only copepods. What would happen if copepods disappeared from the part of the ocean where the herring lived?

A The Newfoundland herring population would eat only sand eels.
B The Newfoundland herring population would eat only arrow worms.
C The Newfoundland herring population would decrease.
D The Newfoundland herring population would increase.

GO ON

Benchmark Test 4

1. Which of these ocean currents carry cold water to warmer areas?

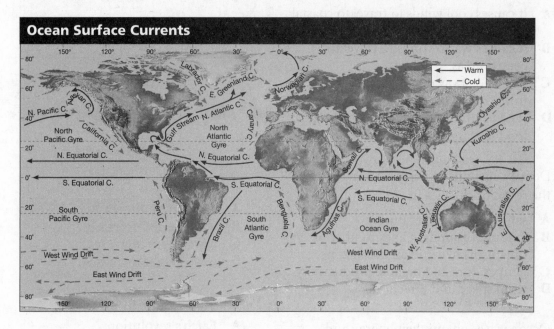

Ocean Surface Currents

A the Peru Current, the California Current, and the W. Australian Current
B the Peru Current, the Brazil Current, and the E. Australian Current
C the W. Australian Current, the California Current, and the N. Pacific Current
D the N. Equatorial Current, the Brazil Current, and the W. Australian Current

2. How do ocean currents help maintain Earth's heat balance?

A They keep warm water near the equator.
B They keep cold water near the poles.
C They move excess heat from the poles toward the tropics.
D They move excess heat from the tropics toward the poles.

3. Which of the following describes the conveyor belt model of ocean circulation?

A Warm water is converted to cold water, thereby releasing heat to the atmosphere.
B Cold water is converted to warm water, thereby releasing heat to the atmosphere.
C Warm water from the poles flows toward the equator to heat the air.
D Cold water from the equator flows toward the poles to heat the air.

GO ON

Benchmark Test 4 (continued)

4. Why is coastal upwelling important to the fishing industries in many areas?

   A It causes cool winds to travel to coastal areas.

   B It causes warm winds to travel to coastal areas.

   C It washes away dead fish and debris from coastal areas.

   D It concentrates nutrients providing food for large populations of fish.

5. Density currents in Earth's oceans form as the result of changes in

   A salinity and temperature.

   B amount of sunlight and number of organisms living in an ocean zone.

   C temperature and organic productivity.

   D wind speed and direction.

6. Ocean waves obtain their energy and motion from the

   A rotation of Earth.

   B wind.

   C sun.

   D collision of ocean currents.

7. The characteristics of a wave are affected by which of the following?

   I. wind speed

   II. length of time the wind has blown

   III. tidal range

   IV. fetch

   A I and II

   B II and III

   C I, II, and IV

   D III only

8. As waves approach the shore, wave speed decreases and

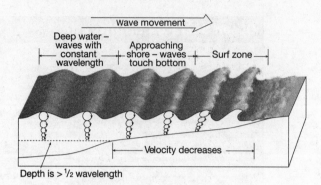

   A wavelength decreases.

   B wave height decreases.

   C wavelength increases.

   D wave height increases.

9. The major influence on tides is

   A Earth's revolution.

   B the sun.

   C the moon.

   D wave motion.

GO ON

10. How does the alignment of Earth, the moon, and the sun shown in the figure affect tides?

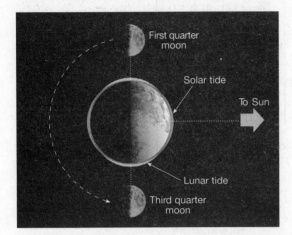

- **A** Low tides are at their highest levels and high tides at their lowest levels.
- **B** High tides are at their highest levels and low tides at their lowest levels.
- **C** Both low and high tides are at their highest levels.
- **D** Both low and high tides are at their lowest levels.

11. Which of the following would result in the most sediment erosion along a shoreline?

- **A** gentle waves in calm weather
- **B** large, high-impact storm waves
- **C** abrasion by sand grains carried by fair-weather waves
- **D** abrasion by sand grains carried in gentle waves

12. The diagram shows waves hitting a shoreline. What area of the shoreline would the wave energy be concentrate, causing greater amounts of erosion?

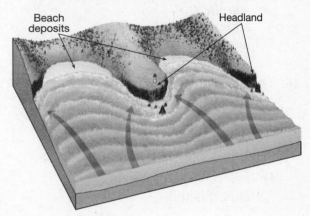

- **A** the beaches
- **B** the bay areas
- **C** the headlands
- **D** Both the bay area and headlands experience the same amount of wave energy.

13. What is a spit?

- **A** a sandbar that forms when the surf selectively erodes rock along a shore
- **B** a ridge of sand that projects from the land into the mouth of an adjacent bay
- **C** a ridge of sand that connects an island to the mainland or other island
- **D** a sandbar that completely crosses a bay

14. Which of the following processes does NOT produce a barrier island?

- **A** isolation of a spit by wave erosion
- **B** deposition followed by an increase in sea level
- **C** deposition by turbulent waters in the line of breakers
- **D** refraction of waves along a headland

GO ON

Benchmark Test 4 (continued)

15. What structure is built perpendicular to a shoreline in order to prevent beach erosion?

   A a seawall
   B a groin
   C a breakwater
   D a tombolo

16. Chlorophyll in green plants

   A reradiates solar energy.
   B absorbs solar energy for photosynthesis.
   C scatters solar energy back into space.
   D reflects solar energy into the atmosphere.

Directions: *Use the image below to answer Question 17.*

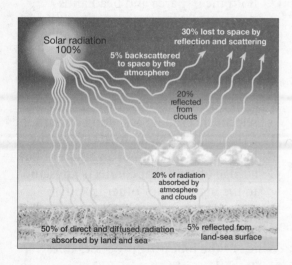

17. How much of incoming solar radiation is reflected back into space from clouds?

   A 5%
   B 20%
   C 30%
   D 50%

18. Changes in Earth's ozone layer are caused by

   A seasonal changes in the number of daylight hours.
   B certain human activities.
   C volcanic eruptions.
   D all of the above

19. What are the major gases in a volume of clean, dry air from MOST abundant to LEAST abundant?

   A oxygen, nitrogen, carbon dioxide, argon
   B nitrogen, oxygen, argon, carbon dioxide
   C argon, carbon dioxide, oxygen, nitrogen
   D carbon dioxide, argon, oxygen, nitrogen

20. What is weather?

   A the extremes of rainfall and temperature for a region
   B the state of the atmosphere at any given time and place
   C the conditions in the stratosphere at a given time.
   D The weather averages for an area collected over many years.

GO ON

Benchmark Test 4 (continued)

21. From the diagram of Earth below, what season would be occurring in South America at this time?

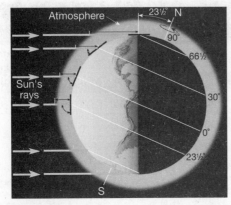

A winter
B spring
C summer
D autumn

22. What is the measure of the average kinetic energy of the molecules in a substance?

A temperature
B convection
C radiation
D heat

23. What mechanism of energy transfer is labeled B in the diagram?

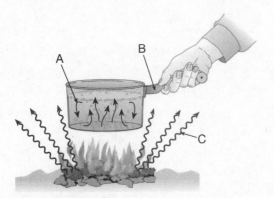

A convection
B radiation
C reflection
D conduction

24. What mechanism of energy transfer can travel through the vacuum of space?

A convection
B radiation
C reflection
D conduction

25. How is most energy transferred in the upper layers of the atmosphere?

A by radiation
B by convection
C by reflection
D by conduction

26. Which of the following factors does **NOT** have a strong influence on the temperature of an area?

A latitude
B altitude
C ocean currents
D longitude

27. What is the major factor that makes the yearly tempertures in Vancouver, Canada, milder than the temperatures in Winnipeg?

A differences in latitude between the two cities
B differences in longitude between the two cities
C more daylight hours in Winnipeg
D location of Vancouver closer to the Pacific Ocean

GO ON

Benchmark Test 4 (continued)

28. Why do many clouds reflect a great deal of the sun's energy back into space?

    A clouds have a low albedo
    B clouds have zero albedo
    C clouds have a high albedo
    D clouds absorb all the sun's energy

29. What is the most important gas in the atmosphere that is involved in vital weather processes?

    A oxygen
    B carbon dioxide
    C water vapor
    D nitrogen

30. Which of the following processes involved in a change of state results in a release of heat?

    A freezing
    B melting
    C evaporation
    D changing a liquid to a gas

31. From the data table below, how much water vapor is needed to saturate the air at 20 degrees Celsius?

Water Vapor Needed for Saturation		
Temperature		Mass of water vapor per kg of air (g/kg)
°C	(°F)	
−40	(−40)	0.1
−30	(−22)	0.3
−20	(−4)	0.75
−10	(14)	2
0	(32)	3.5
5	(41)	5
10	(50)	7
15	(59)	10
20	(68)	14
25	(77)	20
30	(86)	26.5
35	(95)	35
40	(104)	47

    A 0.3 g/kg
    B 0.75 g/kg
    C 14 g/kg
    D 47 g/kg

GO ON

Benchmark Test 4 (continued)

32. Which of the following statements is true for relative humidity?

 A It is the actual quantity of moisture in the air.
 B Cold air can hold more moisture, so has a higher relative humidity.
 C Warm air can hold less moisture, so has a lower relative humidity.
 D Relative humidity indicates how near the air is to saturation.

33. When the water-vapor content of air remains constant, raising air temperature

 A causes a decrease in relative humidity.
 B causes an increase in relative humidity.
 C has no effect on the relative humidity.
 D causes great fluctuations in relative humidity.

34. When air is compressed, it warms because the air molecules

 A become unstable.
 B rise above the troposphere.
 C spread apart, resulting in fewer collisions.
 D move together, resulting in more collisions.

35. Which of the following processes is caused by a geographic obstruction such as mountains?

 A orographic lifting
 B frontal wedging
 C convergence
 D monsoons

Directions: *Use the image below to answer Question 36.*

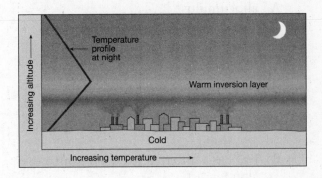

36. What happens during a temperature inversion?

 A Warm air overlying cooler air acts like a lid, preventing upward movement of air.
 B Cold air overlying warmer air act like a lid, preventing upward movement of air.
 C Radiation from the ground causes a rapid warming of the surface.
 D Convection in the air causes rapid mixing of gases in the air.

37. For fog, dew, or clouds to form by condensation what condition must the air meet?

 A It must be stable.
 B It must be saturated.
 C It must be unsaturated.
 D It must be warm and above the dew point.

Benchmark Test 4

GO ON

38. Which of the following clouds would be classified as a high level cloud?

  A altocumulus
  B cirrus
  C stratocumulus
  D nimbostratus

39. What is different between a cloud and fog?

  A Fog does not have the same structure as a cloud.
  B Fog has a different make up from a cloud.
  C Fog forms at or near the ground surface.
  D Fog looks very different from clouds.

40. What process in warm clouds results in precipitation?

  A Small water drops in the cloud grow by colliding and coalescing with other drops until they are large enough to fall as precipitation.
  B Large water drops in the cloud are broken apart by collisions with other drops until they are small enough to fall as precipitation.
  C Water drops in the cloud are reduced in volume by about one million times until they are small enough to fall as precipitation.
  D Small water drops grow around particles of snow or ice until they are large enough to fall as precipitation.

41. Sleet forms when

  A a layer of warm air is found near the surface.
  B a layer of air above freezing overlies a layer below freezing near the ground.
  C the lower atmosphere is below freezing all the way to the ground.
  D updrafts in the clouds carry ice pellets upwards forming a layer of ice.

42. The air pressure exerted on an object

  A by pushing down on the object is greater than the air pressure pushing up on the object.
  B is the same in all directions.
  C by pushing down on the object is less than the air pressure pushing up on the object.
  D has no effect upon the object.

43. Which instrument is used to measure air pressure?

  A spectrometer
  B altimeter
  C barometer
  D thermometer

GO ON

Benchmark Test 4 (continued)

44. From the map below in what direction is the wind blowing in Illinois at the location labeled with a "L"?

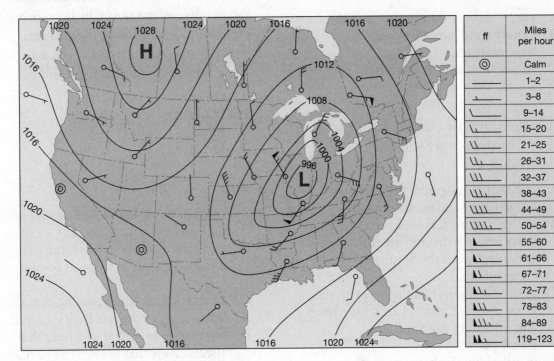

ff	Miles per hour
⊙	Calm
—	1–2
⌐	3–8
⌐	9–14
⌐	15–20
⌐	21–25
⌐	26–31
⌐	32–37
⌐	38–43
⌐	44–49
⌐	50–54
⌐	55–60
⌐	61–66
⌐	67–71
⌐	72–77
⌐	78–83
⌐	84–89
⌐	119–123

A The wind is blowing toward the south only.
B The wind is blowing toward the west only.
C The wind is blowing outward, away from the L.
D The wind is blowing inward, toward the L.

45. In what direction does the Coriolis effect cause winds to be deflected in the Northern Hemisphere?

A to the right of their path of motion
B to the left of their path of motion
C The Coriolis effect does not deflect winds in the Northern Hemisphere.
D towards the north

46. As a result of the Coriolis effect, winds in pressure centers in the Southern Hemisphere blow

A counterclockwise around a low and clockwise around a high.
B clockwise around a low and counterclockwise around a high.
C inward around an anticyclone.
D outward around a cyclone.

GO ON

Benchmark Test 4 (continued)

47. Centers of high pressure are frequently associated with

   A sunny skies and heavy precipitation.
   B cloudy conditions and high temperatures.
   C sunny skies and dry weather.
   D cloudy skies and precipitation.

48. How does air flow around an anticyclone in the Northern and Southern Hemispheres?

   A in either hemisphere the air flows outward around an anticyclone
   B in the Northern Hemisphere the air flows inwards around an anticyclone, and outward in the Southern Hemisphere
   C in the Northern Hemisphere the air flows outward around an anticyclone, and inward in the Southern Hemisphere
   D in either hemisphere the air flows inward around an anticyclone

49. What causes circulation patterns in Earth's oceans and atmosphere?

   A convection in Earth's core
   B movements of tectonic plates
   C uniform heating of Earth's surface
   D uneven heating of Earth's surface

50. What is a sea breeze?

   A a nighttime breeze in which warm air moves toward the sea
   B a daytime breeze in which cool air moves toward the land
   C a daytime breeze in which warm air moves toward the land
   D a nighttime breeze in which cool air moves toward the sea

51. You live in Indiana, and you want to know what the weather will most likely be for the next couple of days. At which neighboring state should you look at the current weather conditions to help forecast your likely weather for the near future?

   A Ohio
   B Kentucky
   C Illinois
   D Michigan

52. What is El Niño?

   A an episode of ocean cooling that affects the eastern tropical Pacific Ocean
   B an episode of ocean warming that affects the eastern tropical Pacific Ocean
   C an episode of global cooling that affects lands that border the Pacific Ocean
   D an episode of global warming that affects lands that border the Pacific Ocean

53. What is an air mass?

   A a high pressure center where the winds blow clockwise
   B a low pressure center where the winds blow counterclockwise
   C a huge body of air that has similar temperture and moisture characteristics at any given altitude
   D a boundary between two masses of air with different temperature and moisture characteristics

54. Air masses are classified by temperature and

   A their characteristic wind directions.
   B the time of year they form.
   C the surface over which they form.
   D their characteristic wind speeds.

GO ON

Benchmark Test 4 (continued)

55. From the map shown below, what type of air mass influencies most of the weather in the southeastern United States?

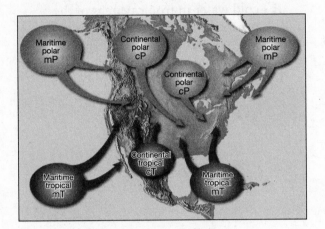

    A   a maritime polar air mass
    B   a continental tropical air mass
    C   a continental polar air mass
    D   a maritime tropical air mass

56. Which two types of air masses are responsible for most of the weather in the United States, east of the Rocky Mountains?

    A   maritime polar and maritime tropical air masses
    B   maritime tropical and continental polar air masses
    C   continental tropical and continental polar air masses
    D   continental tropical and maritime polar air masses

57. What type of front is shown in the image below?

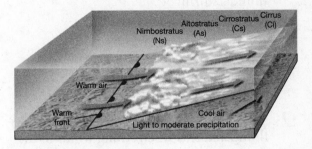

    A   a warm front
    B   a cold front
    C   an occluded front
    D   a stationary front

58. What type of front will form when a cold front overtakes a warm front?

    A   cold front
    B   occluded front
    C   stationary front
    D   warm front

59. Light-to-moderate rains over a large area, for an extended period of time are **most** often associated with which type of front?

    A   cold front
    B   warm front
    C   stationary front
    D   occluded front

GO ON

Benchmark Test 4 (continued)

60. Downdrafts, or downward movements of air throughout a thundercloud cloud are characteristic of which stage of a thunderstorm?

   A cumulus
   B mature
   C updraft
   D dissipating

61. Tornadoes are often associated with severe thunderstorms when strong winds in the upper atmosphere form rotating vertical columns of air called

   A anticyclones.
   B updrafts.
   C mesocyclones.
   D cyclones.

62. What provides the heat and moisture for hurricanes?

   A cold water in polar areas of the oceans
   B cold water in tropical areas of the oceans
   C warm water in tropical areas of the oceans
   D winds blowing off cold land areas

STOP

Benchmark Test 5

1. The two most important elements of climate are

   A elevation and topography.
   B global winds and topography.
   C temperature and vegetation.
   D temperature and precipitation.

2. Which of the following locations would receive the least amount of solar radiation?

   A Albuquerque, New Mexico at about 35 degrees N latitude
   B New Orleans, Louisiana at about 30 degrees N latitude
   C Seward, Alaska at about 60 degrees N latitude
   D Hanamaulu, Hawaii at about 21 degrees N latitude

3. The windward side of a mountain will generally be

   A cool and moist.
   B cool and dry.
   C warm and moist.
   D warm and dry.

4. The climates of inland areas are different from those of coastal areas at the same latitude. Inland climates have

   A cooler summers and colder winters.
   B cooler summers and milder winders.
   C warmer summers and colder winters.
   D warmer summers and milder winters.

5. What mechanism affects climate by distributing heat energy and moisture around the planet?

   A differences in topography
   B differences in elevation
   C differences in latitude
   D global winds systems

6. Two areas are located close to one another at the same latitude. One area has lush forests and the second area has scattered grasses and small shrubs. Which area receives more precipitation?

   A Both areas receive the same amount of precipitation.
   B The forested area receives more precipitation.
   C The area with grasses and shrubs receives more precipitation.
   D The forested area receives less precipitation.

7. Which of the following climates described in the Koppen climate classification system would have cool, rainy winters?

   A polar climate
   B humid tropical climate
   C dry climate
   D humid mid-latitude climate

GO ON

8. The graph below represents an area with a humid tropical climate. What characteristics does this climate have?

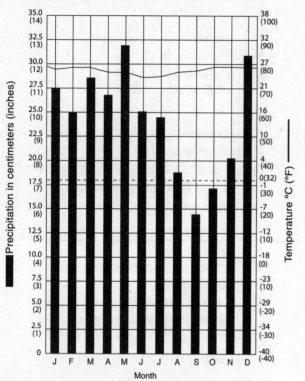

A high tempertures and low amounts of precipitation throughout the year

B high temperatures and high amount of precipitation throughout the year

C low temperatures and low amounts of precipitation throughout the year

D low temperatures and high amounts of precipitation throughout the year

9. The three graphs show the temperatures and amounts of precipitation that are characteristic of humid mid-latitude climates. Note: the bars represent precipitation and the lines represent temperature. In which three months does Cape Town, South Africa, recieve the most precipitation?

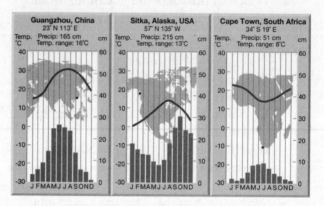

A May, June, and July

B June, July, and August

C January, February, and March

D September, October, adn November

10. Deserts are characterized by

A high rainfall and high temperatures.

B low rainfall and high rates of evaporation.

C low rainfall and low rates of evaporation.

D low temperatures and high rainfall.

GO ON

Benchmark Test 5 (continued)

11. What is the main characteristic of polar climates?

    A the mean temperature of the warmest month is below 10 degrees Celsius
    B the mean temperature of the coldest month is below 20 degrees Celsius
    C the mean temperature of the warmest month is above 20 degrees Celsius
    D the mean temperature of the coldest month is below 50 degrees Celsius

12. How would the climate of a highland area compare with that of an area nearby that is at a lower elevation?

    A the highland area would have a warmer and dryer climate
    B the lowland area would have a cooler and dryer climate
    C the lowland area would have a warmer and wetter climate
    D the highland area would have a cooler and wetter climate

13. Which of the following is NOT an example of a natural process that causes climate change?

    A volcanic eruptions
    B ocean circulation
    C solar activity
    D moon phases

14. Why is the greenhouse effect important?

    A Without it, Earth's oceans would not exist.
    B Without it, tectonic plates would not move over Earth's surface.
    C Without it, Earth would be uninhabitable.
    D Without it, Earth would have no atmosphere.

Directions: *Use the graph below to answer Question 15.*

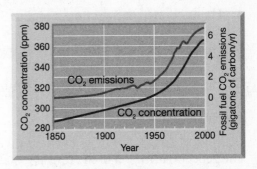

15. How do carbon dioxide (CO_2) emissions from burning fossil fuels and concentrations of this gas in the air compare for the time shown?

    A Emissions greatly increased while concentrations of the gas decreased.
    B Concentrations of the gas greatly increased while emissions decreased.
    C As emissions increased, so did the concentrations of the gas.
    D As emissions decreased, so did the concentrations of the gas.

16. As a result of increases in carbon dioxide and other gases in the air, global temperatures have risen in what is called global warming. Climate modeling has suggested that as a result of global warming,

    A more water vapor will enter the air.
    B sea level will rise and cause erosion and flooding.
    C drastic changes in weather patterns will occur.
    D all of the above.

GO ON

Benchmark Test 5 (continued)

17. What major discovery did the Greek philosopher Aristotle make in Earth science?

   A He calculated the circumference of Earth.
   B He developed a model for predicting lunar eclipses.
   C He concluded that Earth was round, instead of flat.
   D He developed a star catalog.

18. The geocentric model of the universe states that

   A the planets move in retrograde motion around the sun.
   B Earth and the other planets orbit the sun.
   C the orbit of Jupiter lies between the sun and Earth.
   D the sun and the planets orbit Earth.

19. The Earth-centered view of the universe was dominant for nearly 2000 years. The astronomer credited with changing that view to a sun-centered model was

   A Ptolemy.
   B Sagan.
   C Kepler.
   D Copernicus.

20. What motion of Earth results in the planet spinning on its axis?

   A precession
   B rotation
   C revolution
   D perihelion

21. Which position in the diagram below would the moon be in during the full moon phase?

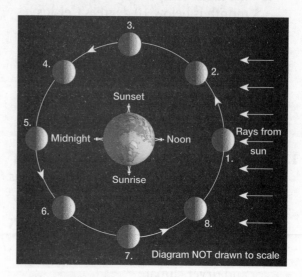

   A position 1
   B position 3
   C position 5
   D position 7

22. A total lunar eclipse occurs when

   A the moon is between Earth and the sun.
   B the entire moon is within Earth's umbra.
   C part of the moon is within Earth's umbra.
   D part of the moon is within Earth's penumbra.

23. How have asteroid impacts affected many of the bodies in our solar system?

   A The impacts have created surface craters.
   B The impacts have caused rock to be ejected from the surfaces of the objects struck.
   C The impacts have sent dust into the air, which blocked the sun and, on Earth, caused extinctions.
   D all of the above.

GO ON

Benchmark Test 5 (continued)

24. What technique did scientists use to determine that the moon's maria basalts are between 3.2 billion and 3.8 billion years old?

A cross correlation with index fossils
B radiometric dating
C observing variations in crater density
D comparing the color of the moon's basalts with basalts on Earth

Directions: *Use the chart below to answer Question 25.*

Period of Revolution and Solar Distances of Planets		
Planet	**Solar Distance (AU)***	**Period (Earth years)**
Mercury	0.39	0.24
Venus	0.72	0.62
Earth	1.00	1.00
Mars	1.52	1.88
Jupiter	5.20	11.86
Saturn	9.54	29.46
Uranus	19.18	84.01
Neptune	30.06	164.80
Pluto	39.44	247.70

*AU = astronomial unit

25. Based on the data in the table, how far is Mercury from the sun in kilometers?

A 4.4 billion kilometers
B 5.9 billion kilometers
C 58.5 million kilometers
D 0.39 million kilometers

26. Evidence from Earth and moon rocks suggests that our solar system formed about

A 4.6 million years ago from a rotating cloud of gas and dust.
B 4.6 million years ago from an enormous explosion.
C 4.6 billion years ago from an enormous explosion.
D 4.6 billion years ago from a rotating cloud of gas and dust.

27. Which statement **BEST** explains why scientists are eager to conduct more in-depth studies of Mars?

A Mars has a thin atmosphere.
B Liquid water may have once flowed on Mars's surface.
C Mars is relatively close to Earth.
D Mars has seasons, much like Earth.

28. Which of the following is true of Jupiter, Saturn, Uranus, and Neptune?

A They all have about a dozen satellites.
B They all have ring systems.
C They all rotate on their "sides."
D They all have cratered surfaces.

29. Why is Pluto not classified as a planet?

A It is too far from the sun.
B It does not have any moons in orbit around it.
C It has not cleared debris from the area around its orbit.
D It is not spherical.

GO ON

30. Where are most asteriods found within our solar system?

   A between the orbits of Neptune and Uranus

   B between the orbits Earth and Mars

   C between the orbits of Mars and Jupiter

   D between the orbits of Jupiter and Saturn

31. What part of a comet is labeled A in the diagram below?

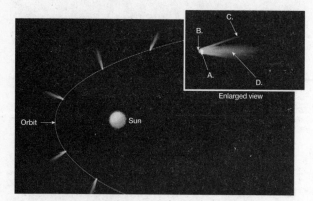

   A the coma

   B the tail

   C the nucleus

   D the nebula

32. Which of the following would be the MOST likely origin for a meteoroid that impacts the planet Mars?

   A debris orbiting within Saturn's ring system

   B the asteroid belt

   C material expelled from the sun by solar flares

   D solid remains of a comet in the outer solar system

33. What type of electromagnetic radiation from the sun has the shortest wavelengths?

   A visible light

   B gamma rays

   C infrared rays

   D radio waves

34. What can scientists determine by studying the spectral lines from the spectrum of a star?

   A the star's size

   B the star's distance from Earth

   C the star's mass

   D the star's chemical composition

35. When using the apparent change in wavelength of a star using the Doppler effect, what can scientists determine about the star if the wavelenth of light has shifted a large amount toward the red end of the spectum?

   A The star is moving away from Earth at a high speed.

   B The star is moving away from Earth at a very low speed.

   C The star is moving toward Earth at a high speed.

   D The star is moving toward Earth at a very low speed.

GO ON

Benchmark Test 5 (continued)

36. What type of telescope is shown in the diagram below?

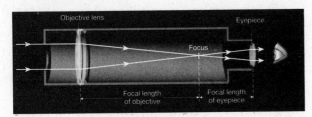

- **A** a radio telescope
- **B** a refracting telescope
- **C** a reflection telescope
- **D** the Hubble Space Telescope

37. What type of Earth-based telescope can detect gas clouds too cool to emit visible light and are less affected by Earth's weather?

- **A** a refracting telescope
- **B** an X-ray telescope
- **C** a reflecting telescope
- **D** a radio telescope

38. What kind of information do visual telescopes like the Hubble Space Telescope provide about star life cycles?

- **A** They collect gamma rays given off by exploding stars that are about half way through their life cycles.
- **B** They provide images that show star color, which is a clue to a star's temperature.
- **C** They gather X-rays given off by black holes, the end points of many stars.
- **D** They map the galactic distribution of hydrogen, which is the main material from which stars are made.

Directions: *Use the diagram below to answer Question 39.*

Structure of the Sun

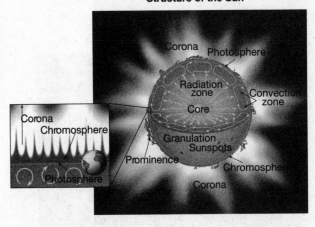

39. Which layers of the sun form the solar atmosphere?

- **A** core and convection zone
- **B** corona and chromosphere
- **C** chromosphere and photosphere
- **D** photosphere and core

40. Two effects of solar flares are

- **A** global warming and hurricane-force winds.
- **B** disruption of satellite transmissions and a decrease in cumulus clouds.
- **C** magnetic fields and solar eclipses.
- **D** auroras and the disruption of radio communications.

GO ON

Benchmark Test 5 (continued)

41. The process shown in the diagram below takes place in the core of all stars, including our sun. Which answer best describes this process?

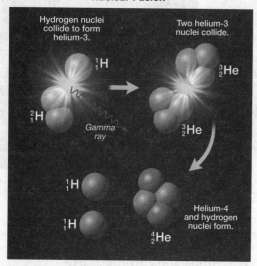

Nuclear Fusion

Hydrogen nuclei collide to form helium-3.

Two helium-3 nuclei collide.

$^1_1$H

$^3_2$He

$^2_1$H

$^3_2$He

Gamma ray

$^1_1$H

$^1_1$H

Helium-4 and hydrogen nuclei form.

$^4_2$He

A New atoms are formed.
B Energy is absorbed.
C New atoms are formed and energy is released.
D Atoms are split and energy is absorbed.

42. What information about a star can be determined from binary stars?

A the star's distance from Earth
B the star's mass
C the star's absolute magnitude
D the star's temperature

43. What two pieces of evidence lead astronomers to conclude that stars are much farther from Earth than the planets in the solar system are?

A nuclear fusion and parallax
B parallax and precession
C parallax and the observation that planets passed in front of stars
D precession and the observation that planets passed behind stars

44. What factors determine a star's apparent magnitude?

A the star's temperature and the star's size only
B the star's temperature, star's size, and distance from Earth
C the star's size, the star's chemical composition, the star's temperature
D the star's color and distance from Earth only

Directions: *Use the graph below to answer Question 45.*

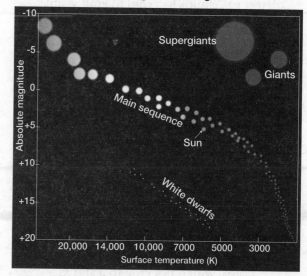

Hertzsprung-Russel Diagram

45. How does the temperature of the sun compare to the temperature range of giants?

A The tempertures of giants cannot be determined.
B Most giants are hotter than the sun.
C Most giants are cooler than the sun.
D Like the sun, giants are main-sequence stars; thus, their temperatures fall into the same range as the sun's temperature.

GO ON

Benchmark Test 5 (continued)

46. Which of the following stages in a star's life cycle marks the birth of a star?

   A planetary nebula stage after a supernova

   B white dwarf whose core begins helium fusion

   C variable stage with core temperatures of less than 10 million K

   D protostar whose core begins nuclear fusion of hydrogen

47. How do massive stars with masses three times or more of the sun's mass die?

   A by expanding to form a supergiant

   B by collapsing into a white dwarf

   C by collapsing into a white dwarf and ejecting a planetary nebula

   D by a supernova explosion

48. When does a star become a main sequence star?

   A when outward pressure on the star equals the inward force of gravity

   B after it has used up all of its fuel and starts to expand outward

   C when it reaches the planetary nebula stage

   D after it explodes as a supernova

49. Where within the Milky Way is our solar system located?

   A in one of the bars

   B in one of the arms

   C in a globular cluster

   D in the nucleus

50. Studies indicate that the largest objects in the universe are probably

   A spiral galaxies.

   B irregular galaxies.

   C groups of galaxies called clusters.

   D groups of galaxies called superclusters.

51. Hubble's study of the red shifts of galaxies indicates the the universe

   A is contracting.

   B maintains a steady state.

   C fluctuates in size

   D is expanding.

52. According to the big bang theory, when did all matter form?

   A prior to the explosion

   B at the time of the explosion

   C about 4.6 billion years ago

   D a few million years ago

STOP

Outcome Test

1. Which of the following is a subdivision of Earth science that deals with the study of Earth's history and Earth processes?

   A biology
   B astronomy
   C geology
   D oceanography

2. Which labeled point shown in the image below is located at 45 degrees north and 75 degrees west?

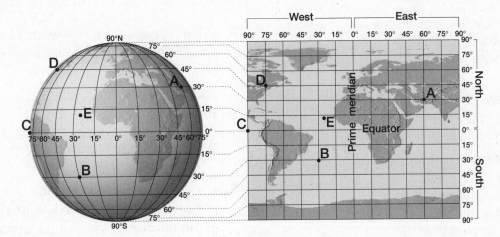

   A Point A
   B Point B
   C Point D
   D Point E

3. Which statement **BEST** describes experiment A?

   > Experiment A was carried out, data were collected, and an explanation for the results was expressed. The experiment was conducted several more times and the results were confirmed.

   A Experiment A supports the hypothesis.
   B Experiment A is inconclusive.
   C Experiment A did not follow proper scientific methods.
   D Experiment A is considered to be a theory.

GO ON

Outcome Test (continued)

4. What type of chemical bonding is shown in the diagram below?

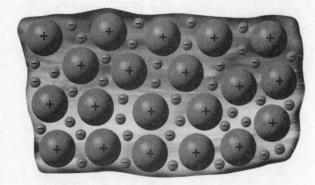

   A ionic bonding
   B covalent bonding
   C metallic bonding
   D isotopic bonding

5. Why would a sugar cube **NOT** be considered to be a mineral?

   A it is not naturally occurring
   B it is not a solid
   C it is not inorganic
   D it is not have a particular chemical composition

6. Minerals that form chains, sheets, and three-dimensional networks are

   A halides.
   B sulfates.
   C carbonates.
   D silicates.

7. How are photosynthesis and respiration related in Earth's carbon cycle?

   A They both put carbon dioxide back into the atmosphere.
   B They both take carbon dioxide from the atmosphere.
   C Photosynthesis removes carbon dioxide from the air and respiration puts this gas back into the air.
   D Respiration removes carbon dioxide from the air and photosynthesis puts this gas back into the air.

8. What type of rock forms when weathered and eroded sediments are compacted and cemented?

   A igneous rock
   B sedimentary rock
   C metamorphic rock
   D foliated rock

9. On a field trip, Jessica found a metamorphic rock which has interlocking grains of calcite. How should Jessica classify this rock?

   A as gneiss
   B as marble
   C as schist
   D as quartzite

10. Which of following is an example of a nonrenewable resource?

   A iron ore used to make steel
   B corn used to make ethanol
   C wheat used to make bread
   D cotton used to make clothing

Outcome Test

GO ON

Outcome Test (continued)

11. The devices shown in the foreground provide some of the electricity used in Sacramento, California. How do these devices work?

A They set wind turbines in motion to produce electricity.
B They change color to indicate when solar output is high.
C They store energy from the tides and convert it to electricity.
D They absorb solar energy and convert it to electricity.

12. What gas in the atmosphere is vital for the existance of most animal life on Earth?

A nitrogen
B oxygen
C argon
D carbon dioxide

13. Which type of soil is commonly found in the drier parts of the western United States that have grasses and brush vegetation?

A humus
B laterite
C pedalfer
D pedocal

14. How do scientists classify a mass movement that consists of a thick fluid that moves rapidly downslope?

A as a mudflow
B as a rockslide
C as creep
D as a rockfall

15. The process of runoff is illustrated by the

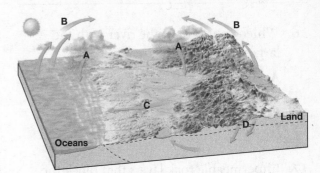

A arrows labeled D.
B arrow labeled C.
C arrows labeled B.
D arrows labeled A.

GO ON

Outcome Test (continued)

Directions: *Use the chart below to answer Question 16.*

Some of the World's Largest Rivers		
River	**Country**	**Average Discharge m³/s**
Ganges	India	18,700
Amazon	Brazil	212,400
Paran	Argentina	14,900
Lena	Russia	15,500
Congo	Zaire	39,650
Orinoco	Venezuela	17,000
Yangtze	China	21,800
Mississippi	United States	17,300
Brahmaputra	Bangladesh	19,800
Yenisei	Russia	17,400

16. Which country has the river with the largest average discharge?

   A India
   B United States
   C Brazil
   D Zaire

17. Impermeable rock layers that block the flow of groundwater are

   A geysers.
   B springs.
   C aquifers.
   D aquitards.

18. What feature caused by glacial erosion is labeled B in the diagram below?

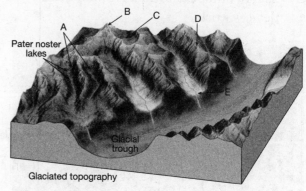

Glaciated topography

   A a cirque
   B a horn
   C an arete
   D a hanging valley

Directions: *Use the diagram below to answer Question 19.*

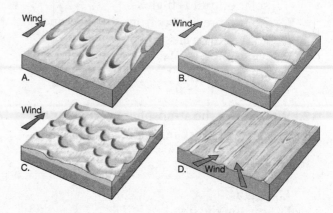

19. What types of sand dunes are illustrated in diagram B?

   A barchan dunes
   B transverse dunes
   C longitudinal dunes
   D barchanoid dunes

GO ON

Outcome Test (continued)

20. What type of seismic waves compress and expand rocks in the direction the waves travel?

   A surface waves
   B P waves
   C S waves
   D transverse waves

21. Which of the following statements is true of earthquakes?

   A Every earthquake causes extensive damage and seismic shaking.
   B Every earthquake has a single moment magnitude but can vary in intensity.
   C Every earthquake measures at least 2.0 on the Richter scale.
   D Every earthquake has foreshocks that occur before the earthquake.

22. Which of the following is **NOT** a hazard associated with an earthquake?

   A flooding of major rivers
   B seismic shaking causing highway overpasses to collapse
   C landslides damaging roads and buildings
   D tsunamis causing coastal flooding and destruction

23. What features are part of the longest mountain range on Earth's surface?

   A deep-ocean trenches
   B mid-ocean ridges
   C subduction zones
   D volcanic island arcs

24. All of the following are evidence of plate tectonics **EXCEPT**

   A magnetic patterns on either side of a mid-ocean ridge.
   B ocean-floor topography.
   C the increase in the age of rocks and sediment with distance from a mid-ocean ridge.
   D the vertical distribution of ocean organisms.

Directions: *Use the diagram below to answer Question 25.*

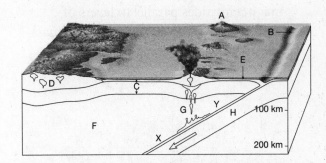

25. The feature illustrated at A in the diagram is

   A a continental volcanic arc.
   B a trench.
   C a volcanic island arc.
   D an oceanic ridge.

26. At which of the following locations would volcanism **NOT** be likely to occur?

   A at a hot spot in the crust
   B at a divergent plate boundary
   C at a continental-continental convergent boundary
   D at a oceanic-oceanic convergent boundary

GO ON

Outcome Test (continued)

27. Which of the following BEST describes shield volcanoes?

   A Shield volcanoes are symmetrical cones composed of lava and pyroclastic deposits.

   B Shield volcanoes erupt fluid lava to form cones with gentle slopes.

   C Shield volcanoes are steep-sided cones composed of cinders.

   D Shield volcanoes are small cones composed of layers of cinders and lava.

28. Which of the intrusive igneous features shown in the diagram are formed when magma intrudes parallel to layers of sedimentary rock to form a bulging mass that forces the overlying rock layers upwards?

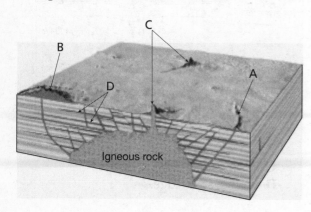

   A dikes

   B laccoliths

   C volcanic necks

   D sills

29. What type of stress squeezes a rock producing a shortening of the rock?

   A compressional stress

   B shear stress

   C tensional stress

   D isostatic stress

30. What type of fault is shown in the diagram?

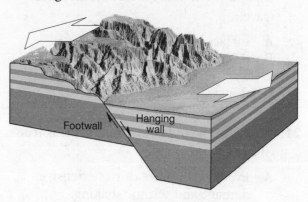

   A a strike-slip fault

   B a reverse fault

   C a thrust fault

   D a normal fault

31. Most mountain building occurs at

   A divergent plate boundaries.

   B hot spots.

   C basins.

   D convergent plate boundaries.

32. Which of the following principles can be applied to interpret the history of these rock layers?

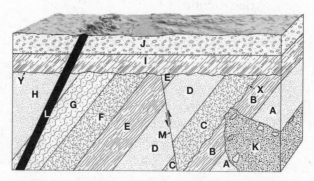

   A law of superposition

   B principle of cross-cutting relationships

   C principle of original horizontality

   D all of the above

GO ON

Outcome Test (continued)

33. What type of fossil would be formed if a brachiopod shell dissolved and that hollow space was later filled by calcite?

   A preserved remains
   B a carbon film
   C a trace fossil
   D a mold and cast fossil

34. List the periods of the Paleozoic Era from oldest to youngest.

   A Cambrian, Ordovician, Silurian, Devonian, Carboniferous, Permian
   B Triassic, Jurassic, Cretaceous
   C Permian, Devonian, Carboniferous, Silurian, Ordovician, Cambrian
   D Cambrian, Devonian, Ordovician, Carboniferous, Permian, Silurian

35. When did a major, rapid diversification of invertebrate organisms to form many new groups occur during the Paleozoic era?

   A during the Ordovician Explosion
   B during the Permian mass extinction
   C during the Cambrian Explosion
   D during the Devonian Explosion

36. What major group first appears in the Mesozoic Era?

   A amphibians
   B reptiles
   C flowering plants
   D land plants

37. Which of the four main ocean basins is labeled B on the map below?

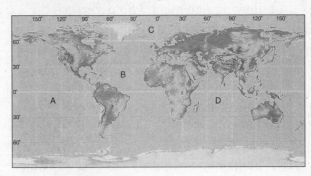

   A Indian Ocean
   B Atlantic Ocean
   C Pacific Ocean
   D Arctic Ocean

38. Which of the following features marks a submerged inactive volcano with an eroded, flat-top on the ocean floor?

   A a plateau
   B a trench
   C an abyssal plain
   D a guyot

39. How would a photosynthetic algae that drifts through the shallow tropical ocean be classified?

   A benthos
   B zooplankton
   C phytoplankton
   D nekton

40. Based on the distance from shore, identify the marine life zone described in the following statement: Photosynthesis occurs, nutrients are abundant, and shelter and habitat are available on the bottom.

   A   intertidal zone
   B   neritic zone
   C   oceanic zone
   D   abyssal zone

41. A long period of high winds over an area of open ocean would have what effect on waves?

   A   Winds have no effect on ocean waves.
   B   there would be no waves
   C   wave heights would be large
   D   wave heights would be small

42. What type of tides are experienced when the sun, moon, and Earth are in the positions shown in the diagram?

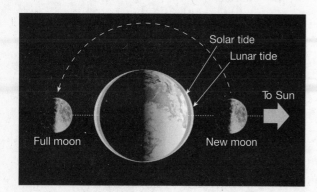

   A   neap tides
   B   spring tides
   C   no tides
   D   tides with the lowest tidal range

43. What mechanism of energy transfer is labeled A in the diagram?

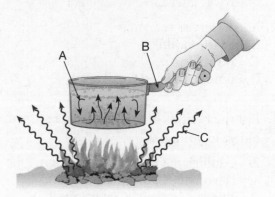

   A   reflection
   B   radiation
   C   convection
   D   conduction

44. Both City A and City B are at the same latitude. Which city would experience greater extremes in temperature throughout the year, City A which is located near the ocean, or City B which is several hundred miles inland from the ocean?

   A   City A and City B would have the same temperature range throughout the year.
   B   City A would have the greater range in temperatures throughout the year.
   C   City B would have the greater range in temperatures throughout the year.
   D   City A and City B would have the same temperature extremes.

GO ON

Outcome Test (continued)

45. What are the four main mechanisms that cause air to rise?

   A orographic lifting, frontal wedging, divergence, and localized convective lifting

   B orographic lifting, frontal wedging, convergence, and localized convective lifting

   C adibatic lifting, frontal wedging, convergence, and localized convective lifting

   D condensation, orographic lifting, frontal wedging, and localized convective lifting

46. Which of the following clouds would be classified as a low level cloud?

   A altocumulus
   B cirrus
   C cirrostratus
   D stratus

47. The path of a rocket fired from a location in northern Canada toward the equator would be deflected to the right. What force causes this deflection in the rocket's path?

   A the orographic effect
   B the Coriolis effect
   C Earth's revolution around the sun
   D atmospheric convection

48. You live in Arkansas, and you want to know what the weather will most likely be for the next couple of days. At which neighboring state should you look at the current weather conditions to help forecast your likely weather for the near future?

   A Missouri
   B Oklahoma
   C Louisiana
   D Mississippi

49. Warm fronts have much lower slopes than cold fronts and advance more slowly. This causes the

   A wind shift from the north to the southwest that is associated with a warm front.

   B violent, long-lasting thunderstorms associated with warm fronts.

   C more violent weather associated with a warm front.

   D light-to-moderate precipitation over a large area for extended periods associated with a warm front.

GO ON

Outcome Test (continued)

50. Which stage of a thunderstorm characterized by heavy rain is shown in the diagram?

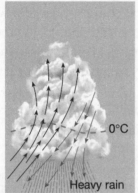

- **A** cumulus
- **B** mature
- **C** downdraft
- **D** dissipating

51. Why is the climate of some coastal areas warm even at mid or high latitudes?

- **A** Winds blow warm air toward the ocean from warmer areas inland.
- **B** Ocean currents from the tropics warm the air around these areas.
- **C** Water currents from the poles warm up as they flow south.
- **D** all of the above

52. Which of the following processes is *least* likely to cause long-term changes in the Earth's climate?

- **A** major changes in ocean circulation
- **B** changes in Earth's tilt on its axis
- **C** a long period of volcanic eruptions
- **D** changes in the 11-year cycle of sunspots

53. What position in the diagram below would the moon be in during the first quarter phase?

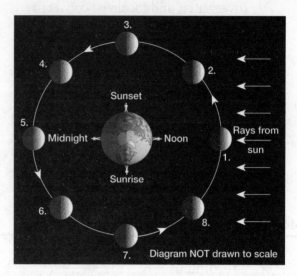

- **A** position 1
- **B** position 4
- **C** position 5
- **D** position 3

54. Which of the following best explains the absence of widespread weathering and erosion on the moon?

- **A** The moon has a very dense atmosphere.
- **B** The moon has little to no surface water.
- **C** The moon's surface is protected by Earth.
- **D** The moon is too far from the sun for weathering and erosion to occur.

GO ON

Outcome Test (continued)

Directions: *Use the chart below to answer Question 55.*

Comparison of the Atmospheres and Surface Temperatures of Mercury, Venus, Earth, Mars					
Planet or Body	**Gases (% by volume)**			**Surface Temperature (range)**	**Surface Atmospheric Pressure (bars)**
	N_2	**O_2**	**CO_2**		
Mercury	0	trace	0	−173° to 427° C	10^{-15}
Venus	3.5	< 0.01	96.5	475° C (small range)	92
Earth	78.01	20.95	0.03	−40° to 75° C	1.014
Mars	2.7	1.3	95.32	−120° to 25° C	0.008

55. The planet with the greatest temperature extremes and very little atmosphere is

    A Earth.
    B Mars.
    C Venus.
    D Mercury.

56. The most volcanically active bodies in our solar system are Earth, Neptune's moon Triton, and

    A Earth's moon.
    B Saturn's moon Titan.
    C Pluto's moon Charon.
    D Jupiter's moon Io.

57. Brief outbursts that appear as a sudden brightening of the region above a dark area in the sun's surface are called

    A coronas.
    B prominences.
    C solar flares.
    D sunspots.

58. The sun is primarily powered by fusion of

    A helium to oxygen.
    B carbon to oxygen.
    C hydrogen to helium.
    D lithium to uranium.

59. What determines the stages of a star's life cycle?

    A the star's initial diameter
    B the star's initial mass
    C the star's apparent magnitude
    D the star's distance from Earth

60. Galaxies are groups of billions of stars that

    A appear as several different types.
    B are held together by gravity.
    C form superclusters.
    D all of the above

STOP

Practice Test 1

1. Which of the following is an example of a nonmetallic mineral resource needed to manufacture a product used in our society?

   A iron used in making steel
   B copper used to make electrical wiring
   C sulfur used in making fertilizers
   D silver used in making jewelry

2. What is the source of geothermal energy?

   A in-and-out flow of ocean tides used to power turbines
   B underground reservoirs of hot water or steam from recent volcanic activity
   C wind energy that is used to turn turbines
   D solar radiation used in photovoltaic cells in solar panels

3. Which of the following could trigger a mass movement on a slope?

   A earthquake near the area
   B unusually low amounts of rainfall in the area
   C planting ground cover and other types of vegetation on the slope
   D unusually high winds in the area

4. What is the location of the epicenter of the earthquake from the travel-time data plotted on the diagram below?

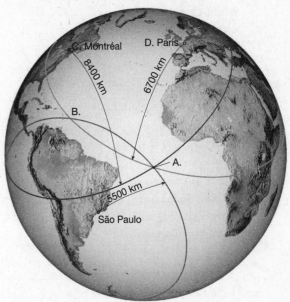

   A location A in the Atlantic Ocean
   B location B just north of South America
   C location C near Montreal
   D location D near Paris

5. Which of the following is an example of how humans use freshwater resources?

   A drinking and cooking
   B washing clothes and dishes
   C to irrigate crops and water livestock
   D All of the above.

6. Which of the following could potentially contaminate groundwater supplies?

   A leaking sewage from septic tanks
   B farm wastes washing off fields
   C leaking underground oil or chemical tanks
   D All of the above.

GO ON

Practice Test 1 (continued)

7. What type of eruption could be expected from a volcano with basaltic magma with a low viscosity and low gas content?

A very explosive eruption
B quiet eruption
C explosive eruption
D moderate eruption

8. The nitrogen cycle is important to all of Earth's organisms because

A nitrogen-fixing bacteria in the soil turn nitrogen gas into ammonia.
B plants and animals cannot use nitrogen gas that is present in the air.
C nitrifying bacteria change ammonia into nitrates, which are used by plants.
D all of the above

9. Lucia finds a rock with interlocking white and black crystals. The rock has no bands or layers. What kind of rock did she find, and how did it form?

A metamorphic; mountain building
B sedimentary; deposition by ice
C igneous; quick cooling of lava
D igneous; slow cooling of magma

10. A rock with rounded pebbles that are held together by a sandy matrix can form

A during mountain building.
B in an ocean or lake.
C deep within the crust.
D during a volcanic eruption.

Growth of World Population

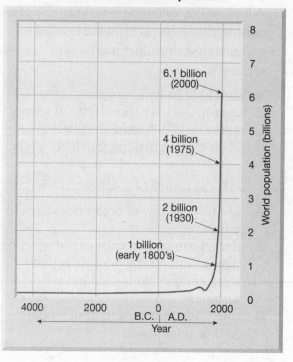

6.1 billion (2000)
4 billion (1975)
2 billion (1930)
1 billion (early 1800's)

11. Which statement is supported by the population graph?

A The population of the world has remained steady for the past two thousand years.
B The world's population has increased dramatically over the past 200 years.
C The world's population peaked in 2000 and is now in decline.
D The world's population has always increased and has never decreased.

GO ON

Practice Test 1 (continued)

Directions: *Use the illustration below to answer Questions 12 and 13.*

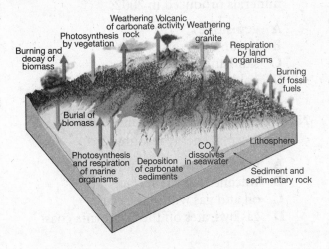

12. Which of these processes in the carbon cycle adds carbon to Earth's atmosphere?

   A respiration

   B photosynthesis

   C deposition of carbonates in the ocean

   D burial of biomass

13. All of these processes remove carbon dioxide from Earth's atmosphere except

   A weathering of granite.

   B photosynthesis.

   C weathering of carbonates by water.

   D decay of biomass.

14. Oil and natural gas are all energy sources formed from

   A plant and animal material that has been transformed over millions of years.

   B nuclear decay of unstable radioactive substances.

   C hydrothermal energy that has been absorbed by underground rock.

   D materials ejected by the sun before life appeared on Earth.

15. How does the amount of solar energy that reaches Earth compare to the energy used by human activities?

   A The solar energy that reaches Earth every second is 10,000 times the amount of energy used by humans in a day.

   B The solar energy that reaches Earth every day is 10,000 times the amount of energy used by humans in a second.

   C The solar energy that reaches Earth every second is 10 times the amount of energy used by humans in a year.

   D The solar energy that reaches Earth every year is 10 times the amount of energy used by humans in a second.

Directions: *Use the diagram to answer Questions 16 and 17.*

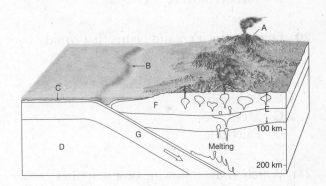

16. What is the feature labeled A, and how does it form?

   A trench; subduction of the oceanic plate

   B continental volcanic arc; melting of the subducting plate

   C volcanic island arc; melting of continental plate

   D folded mountain range; convergence of two continental plates

GO ON

Practice Test 1 (continued)

17. What type of plate boundary is shown?

    A oceanic-continental
    B oceanic-oceanic
    C continental-continental
    D transform fault

18. The sun produces energy through nuclear fusion, converting

    A hydrogen into helium.
    B helium into hydrogen.
    C oxygen into carbon.
    D carbon into oxygen.

19. Which substance was not originally found in Earth's atmosphere?

    A water vapor
    B oxygen
    C nitrogen
    D carbon dioxide

20. During which era did plants that could survive on land first evolve?

    A Cenozoic
    B Precambrian
    C Mesozoic
    D Paleozoic

21. Which of the following best describes Earth just after its formation?

    A a large, gaseous sphere with many moons
    B a small, hot molten sphere
    C a small sphere with a solid core
    D a large gaseous sphere with a dense atmosphere

22. Which economic mineral accounted for the largest part of the total value of minerals produced in 2002?

    A gemstones
    B boron minerals
    C sand and gravel
    D gold and silver

23. What is the source of California's geothermal energy resources?

    A magma close to the surface
    B volcanoes at the surface
    C oil and gas within the crust
    D gas hydrates off the California coast

24. Earthquakes are common in California and can result in natural hazards such as

    A tsunamis
    B liquefaction
    C landslides
    D all of the above

25. An earthquake has its epicenter 5 km north of Monterey, California. Where would seismic shaking probably be the most intense?

    A 100 km north of Monterey
    B 50 km south of Monterey
    C 100 km east of Monterey
    D 5 km north of Monterey

26. What is the major source of fresh water used by most Californians?

    A desalinated ocean water
    B groundwater
    C lakes
    D rain and melted snow

GO ON

Practice Test 1 (continued)

27. What are California's water projects?

A government programs to clean up polluted bodies of water

B networks of water storage and distribution systems

C facilities that desalinate ocean water to produce drinking water

D systems of wells that bring fresh water to the surface

28. What setup would best model how soil and water are heated differently? In each case, assume that you will measure the temperatures of both substances after ten minutes.

A Place two beakers of water under different heat sources.

B Place two beakers of soil under the same heat source.

C Place a large beaker of soil and a small beaker of water beneath the same heat source.

D Place two beakers with equal amounts of soil and water under the same heat source.

29. Pesticide washed from farm fields into the water supply is an example of

A point source pollution.

B recycling.

C nonpoint source pollution.

D organic pest control.

30. One of the best known discarded scientific hypotheses is

A tectonic plate movement.

B the Earth-centered model of the universe.

C the water cycle.

D transform fault boundary movement.

$$Na\cdot \;+\; \cdot \ddot{\underset{\cdot\cdot}{Cl}}\colon \;\longrightarrow\; Na^+ \; \colon\!\ddot{\underset{\cdot\cdot}{Cl}}\colon^-$$

31. What does the diagram show?

A sodium gaining an electron from chlorine

B sodium and chlorine bonding without transfer of electrons

C sodium giving up an electron to chlorine

D sodium and chlorine sharing electrons and protons

32. Natural hazards from California's volcanoes include

A liquefaction.

B lava flows.

C tsunamis.

D all of the above

33. When heat is transferred to a glass of ice water, the temperature of the ice water remains at 0° C until all the ice has melted. The ice water's temperature does not rise because

A the ice water must absorb latent heat to break apart the crystal structure of the ice cubes.

B the latent heat strengthens the bonds between the ice molecules.

C the ice cubes release latent heat, which slows down the melting process.

D evaporation and melting must occur simultaneously, otherwise no temperature change occurs.

34. What causes earthquakes?

A the release of built-up energy in rocks

B any movement along a fault

C tsunamis along a coast

D liquefaction

GO ON

Practice Test 1 (continued)

Directions: *Use the illustration below to answer Question 35.*

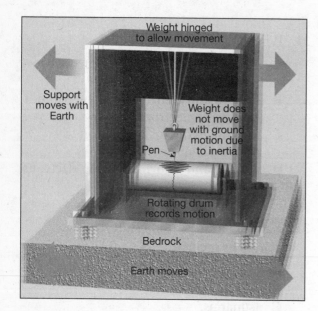

Weight hinged to allow movement

Support moves with Earth

Weight does not move with ground motion due to inertia

Pen

Rotating drum records motion

Bedrock

Earth moves

35. What would a scientist measure with this machine?

   A earthquake magnitude
   B earthquake intensity
   C tsunami height
   D amount of liquefaction

36. Which of the following is probably not a conclusion a geologist could draw using fossils?

   A An area was once covered by water.
   B An area was once near a shoreline.
   C A certain rock layer is older than another.
   D An ancient earthquake with a magnitude of 4.6 struck an area.

37. Heat is distributed around Earth by

   A ocean currents and wind belts.
   B volcanoes and earthquakes.
   C plate motions and tsunami.
   D none of the above.

38. What causes ocean currents and air in pressure centers to move in circular patterns?

   A Earth's revolution
   B Earth's rotation
   C density currents
   D wind in the thermosphere

39. Earth's ozone layer, which is in the stratosphere, is important because it filters

   A UV rays.
   B carbon monoxide.
   C carbon dioxide.
   D nitrogen.

40. Earth's oceans can be divided into distinct layers based on differences in

   A rotation and revolution.
   B volcanoes and earthquakes.
   C salinity and temperature.
   D density and water color.

GO ON

Practice Test 1 (continued)

Directions: *Use the circle graphs below to answer Question 41.*

Primary Pollutants

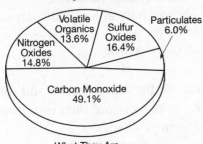

What They Are

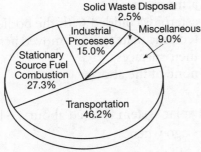

Where They Come From

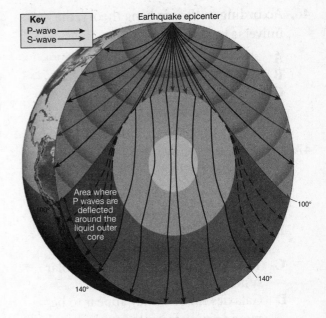

41. Based on the graphs, which of the following is true?

  A Transportation produces all of the carbon monoxide in the air.
  B Nitrogen oxides make up most air pollution.
  C Carbon dioxide makes up most air pollution.
  D Transportation and industrial processes are the cause of most air pollution.

42. Which is **NOT** a method of energy transfer as heat?

  A conduction
  B carbonation
  C radiation
  D convection

43. Which of the following is not true of the waves radiating from the earthquake's epicenter?

  A They are seismic waves.
  B They carry energy.
  C They are strongest far from the epicenter.
  D They are strongest closest to the epicenter.

44. Ocean surface currents are set in motion by

  A Earth's revolution.
  B changes in tides.
  C an increase in salinity.
  D wind moving over the water.

45. Marine organisms are classified based on where they live and how they move. All of the following are marine classifications except

  A plankton.
  B nekton.
  C benthos.
  D auroras.

Practice Test 1 (continued)

46. According to the big bang theory, the universe began

   A about 13.7 million years ago.
   B about 13.7 billion years ago.
   C about 13.7 trillion years ago.
   D about 137,000 years ago.

47. Which of the following is **NOT** one of the reasons that the big bang theory is widely accepted?

   A The universe appears to be expanding.
   B Cosmic background radiation may be left over from the big bang.
   C The sun is at the center of our solar system, not the Earth.
   D Galaxies further away appear to be moving away faster than galaxies which are closer.

Directions: *Use the diagram to answer Question 48.*

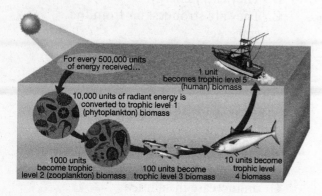

48. The diagram shows that

   A energy flows from trophic level 5 to trophic level 1.
   B energy is transferred efficiently between levels.
   C For every 500,000 units of energy put in, only 1 unit makes it to level 5.
   D The first step in the cycle is trophic level 3.

49. How are Earth, Venus, and Mars similar?

   A They are all Jovian planets.
   B They all formed at about the same time from the same elements.
   C They all have at least one natural satellite.
   D all of the above

50. Craters on the moon, Earth, and some of the other planets and their moons may have formed when

   A meteorites burned up in their atmospheres.
   B asteroids collided with the bodies.
   C tectonic plates slowly moved across their surfaces.
   D none of the above

51. Our solar system formed about 4.6 billion years ago when

   A a cloud of gas and dust contracted and matter became concentrated toward the center of the cloud.
   B an enormous explosion sent matter outward in all directions.
   C nuclear fusion inside the sun's core began to form the known elements.
   D a red giant collapsed and cast off its outer layer to create a cloud of gas.

52. The Milky Way is a spiral galaxy with our solar system located in

   A the center of the galaxy.
   B one of the arms of the galaxy.
   C at the very edge of the galaxy.
   D in the core of the galaxy.

53. Stars that are much more massive than our sun eventually

   A burn out completely.
   B evolve into main sequence stars.
   C explode in a supernova.
   D change into planetary nebulae.

GO ON

Practice test 1 (continued)

54. Which of the following is **NOT** one of the laws governing radiation?

   A Objects that are good absorbers of radiation are good emitters as well.

   B All objects, of any temperature, emit radiant energy.

   C In order for radiant heat to be transferred, either conduction or convection must take place.

   D Hotter objects radiate more total energy per unit area than colder objects do.

Directions: *Use the illustration to answer Question 55.*

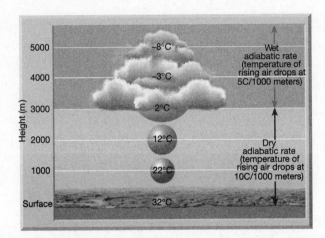

55. What happens at a height of 3000 meters above the surface?

   A The latent heat increases.

   B The rising air cools to its dew point.

   C The rising air becomes compressed.

   D The water vapor in the rising air evaporates.

56. What two forces control the evolution of a star?

   A gravitational collapse and evaporation

   B centripetal force and fusion

   C fission and expansion

   D fusion and gravitational collapse

57. The big bang model suggests that

   A all stars explode as supernovae.

   B the sun is an average star.

   C the universe is expanding.

   D stars are made of burning gases.

58. The universe formed approximately

   A 4.6 million years ago.

   B 4.6 billion years ago.

   C 1 million years ago.

   D 13.7 billion years ago.

STOP

Name _____ Date _____ Class _____

1. Which of following is an example of a renewable resource?

   A aluminum ore used to make airplanes
   B petroleum used to manufacture plastics
   C gold used to make jewelry
   D soybeans used to make cooking oil and food items

2. Almost 71 percent of Earth's surface is covered by water. But less than one percent of the water on Earth is fresh water. Where is most of Earth's freshwater?

   A In the Pacific Ocean.
   B In the Indian Ocean.
   C In the Atlantic Ocean.
   D in glaciers, rivers, lakes, and groundwater

3. What are the particles that are thrown out of volcanoes during an eruption called?

   A pahoehoe material
   B clastic material
   C pyroclastic material
   D magma

4. Laterites are a type of soil that commonly forms in

   A dry climates, such as the western United States.
   B hot, wet tropical areas.
   C temperate areas, such as forested areas of the eastern United States.
   D areas that recieve a moderate amount of rainfall.

Directions: *Use the graph to answer Question 5.*

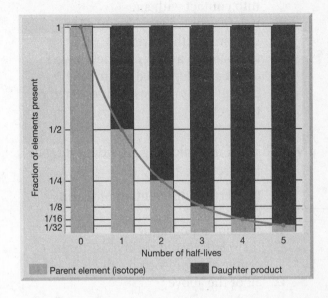

5. If 1/16 of the parent material remains in a sample, how many half-lives have passed?

   A 2
   B 3
   C 4
   D 5

6. Many of the organisms that live in Earth's oceans have a relatively small vertical range in which they can live. This range is defined by

   A temperature.
   B penetration of sunlight.
   C salinity.
   D all of the above

7. Climates differ on either side of a mountain as the result of changes in

   A air circulation and precipitation.
   B cloud cover and temperature.
   C elevation and air pressure.
   D vegetation and elevation.

Practice Test 2

GO ON

Practice Test 2 (continued)

8. A rock with a glassy texture most likely formed when

   A lava cooled very quickly when it came into contact with air.
   B magma cooled very slowly deep beneath Earth's surface.
   C the water in a river channel slowed down and deposited sediment.
   D pressure from opposite sides acted on the rock.

9. Which of the following provides evidence of plate tectonics?

   A the vertical distribution of marine organisms
   B seafloor topography
   C the relatively old rocks close to the center of a mid-ocean ridge
   D all of the above

10. In the Cenozoic Era

    A mammals became the dominant land animals.
    B reptiles became the dominant land animals.
    C amphibians became the dominant land animals.
    D plants moved inland.

11. According to the nebular theory

    A nebulas are composed of 92 percent helium and 7 percent hydrogen.
    B the solar system formed from a rotating cloud of dust and gas.
    C the solar system formed when two large asteroids collided.
    D the terrestrial planets produced the Jovian planets.

12. Earthquake magnitude, as measured on the moment magnitude scale, is the

    A energy released by the earthquake.
    B same as the earthquake's intensity.
    C amount of damage done by the quake.
    D location of the epicenter.

13. Which of the following is NOT true of carbon?

    A In the atmosphere, it is found mainly as carbon dioxide.
    B Coal, oil, and natural gas are compounds made of carbon and hydrogen.
    C Some marine animals use it to produce calcite.
    D Pure carbon is very commonly found in nature.

Directions: *Use the diagram to answer Question 14.*

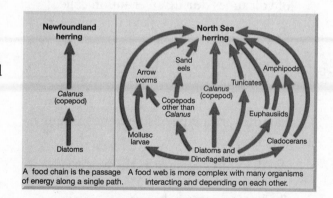

14. According to the diagram, which of the following is true, ?

    A Sand eels depend on the North Sea herring.
    B Diatoms depend on the Newfoundland herring.
    C The North Sea herring only has one source of food.
    D The North Sea herring can feed on amphipods.

GO ON

Practice Test 2 (continued)

15. Which is **NOT** one of California's renewable resources?

    A forest products
    B plants for food
    C natural fibers for clothes
    D natural gas

16. All of the following are effects of El Niño **EXCEPT**

    A greater than average precipitation in the northwestern part of the United States.
    B higher than normal temperatures in the eastern tropical Pacific Ocean.
    C strong undercurrents off the coasts of Peru and Ecuador.
    D greater than normal precipitation in the Gulf Coast states.

17. What are the cause and effect of a temperature inversion?

    A Turbulent wind cause the inversion, which traps warm air under cold air.
    B Lack of air movement causes the inversion, which can trap pollutants close to the ground.
    C Greater than normal precipitation causes an inversion, which can result in flooding.
    D El Niño causes an inversion, which can raise the yield of many crops in northern South America.

18. Where do plants get carbon dioxide for photosynthesis?

    A their cells
    B water molecules
    C the sun
    D the air

19. Earth's rain forests are located

    A at middle latitudes.
    B along ocean shores.
    C in a narrow band along the equator.
    D where the prevailing westerlies form.

20. A geologist finds a fossil in a rock. The fossil seems to be the remains of an organism that scientists think evolved about 440 million years ago, but soon became extinct. The best hypothesis for the scientist to make is that

    A the rock is much less than 440 million years old.
    B the rock is much more than 440 million years old.
    C the rock is around 440 million years old.
    D there is no way to form a hypothesis from this information.

Directions: *Use the diagram to answer Questions 21 and 22.*

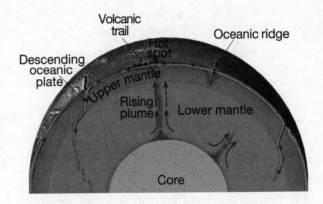

21. A volcanic trail is produced when volcanoes form at a (an)

    A hot spot.
    B descending oceanic plate.
    C oceanic ridge.
    D strike-slip fault.

GO ON

22. The best title for this diagram is

    A "Earth's Core and Mantle."
    B "Earth's Tectonic Plates."
    C "Mantle Convection and Features of Oceanic Crust."
    D "How Batholiths Form."

Directions: *Use the diagram to answer Question 23.*

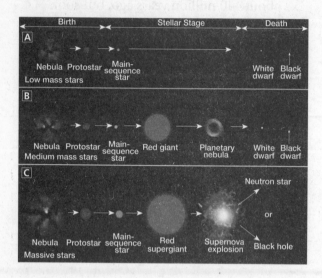

23. Which of the following is true?

    A All stars have a white dwarf phase.
    B A low mass star forms a planetary nebula.
    C Black holes are formed from medium mass stars.
    D A massive star ends its life as a neutron star or a black hole.

24. How is most of the fresh water used in the state of California?

    A for wildlife preserves
    B for recreation
    C for industrial processes
    D to irrigate crops

25. All of the following are natural hazards due to possible volcanic activity on California except

    A volcanic ash.
    B lava flows.
    C carbon dioxide gas.
    D tsunamis.

26. California's most fertile soils are found

    A in the Central Valley.
    B on Mojave Desert.
    C in the wet northern Coast Ranges.
    D on the steep slopes in the Sierra Nevada.

27. If a hypothesis can't be tested,

    A it must be accepted.
    B it is not scientifically useful.
    C it is called a natural hypothesis.
    D it is called an artificial hypothesis.

Directions: *Use the illustration to answer Question 28.*

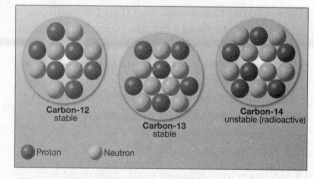

28. Each of the carbon isotopes

    A has six neutrons.
    B has six protons.
    C is radioactive.
    D has the same number of protons and neutrons added together.

GO ON

Practice Test 2 (continued)

29. Which of the following could be caused by an earthquake along California's San Andreas Fault system?

   A landslides
   B liquefaction
   C tsunamis
   D all of the above

30. The greenhouse effect is a process by which

   A certain gases in the air absorb solar radiation to keep Earth's surface at a fairly constant temperature.
   B Earth's surface temperature is dramatically rising as the result of burning fossil fuels.
   C Earth's atmosphere is getting colder, causing short-term changes in weather and climate.
   D none of the above

31. What happens to most of the solar radiation that reaches Earth?

   A It is used by plants to photosynthesize.
   B It is scattered and reflected back into space.
   C It is absorbed by land and water.
   D It is reflected by land and water.

32. Although the neritic zone only covers 5 percent of the oceans, many organisms live there because

   A photosynthesis occurs readily, nutrients wash in from the shore, and the bottom provides shelter.
   B the intense darkness allows animals to protect themselves.
   C high pressures make it easier for slow animals to escape predators.
   D most species have adapted to the waves crashing on the beach.

Directions: *Use the illustration to answer Question 33.*

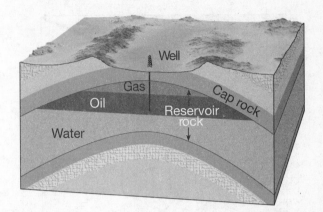

33. The oil did not escape from its reservoir because

   A the cap rock sealed the reservoir.
   B oil does not migrate.
   C the water below kept it in place.
   D the gas prevented it from migrating.

34. Volcanism is associated with all of the following plate boundaries except

   A transform fault boundaries.
   B oceanic-continental convergent boundaries.
   C divergent boundaries.
   D oceanic-oceanic convergent boundaries.

35. Johannes Kepler discovered

   A how to make precise astronomical observations.
   B Earth is a planet orbiting the sun.
   C that matter can be converted to energy.
   D three laws of planetary motion.

GO ON

Practice Test 2 (continued)

Directions: *Use the diagram below to answer Questions 36–38.*

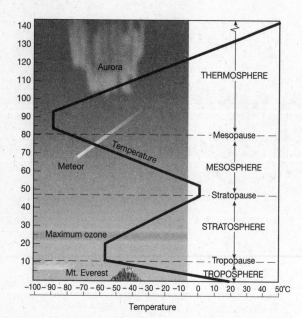

36. In which two layers of Earth's atmosphere do temperatures change in the same manner with height?

  A troposphere and mesosphere
  B troposphere and thermosphere
  C mesosphere and stratosphere
  D stratosphere and mesosphere

37. Where is the ozone layer?

  A about 10 km above Earth's surface
  B about 25 km above Earth's surface
  C about 10 km below the stratopause
  D about 25 km below the mesopause

38. Which layer of the atmosphere is the warmest?

  A troposphere
  B stratosphere
  C mesosphere
  D thermosphere

39. Natural variations in the ozone layer are the result of

  I. seasonal changes.
  II. volcanic eruptions.
  III. human activities.
  IV. changes in precipitation.

  A I only
  B I and II
  C III and IV
  D IV only

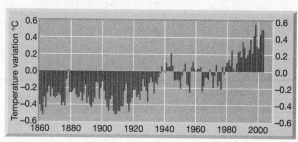

The figure above shows changes in Earth's average surface temperature.

40. According to the figure, which year had the highest average surface temperature on record?

  A 2003
  B 1998
  C 1985
  D 1909
  E 1863

41. What do scientists think may have caused the global warming trend?

  A A decrease in plant life
  B An increase in greenhouse gases in the atmosphere
  C A change in Earth's rotational axis
  D An increase in acid rain
  E A decrease in the ozone layer

GO ON

Practice Test 2 (continued)

42. During a total eclipse of the moon,

  A Earth is completely in the penumbra.
  B Earth is completely in the umbra.
  C the moon is completely in the penumbra.
  D the moon is completely in the umbra.
  E Earth and moon are on opposite sides of the sun.

43. Which of the following bodies in the solar system does not fit easily into either the terrestrial or Jovian planet categories?

  A Earth
  B Uranus
  C Pluto
  D Mercury
  E Mars

44. Most of the sunlight emitted from the sun comes from the

  A photosphere.
  B corona.
  C chromosphere.
  D core.
  E prominence.

45. How did asteroid impacts affect Earth, its moon, and other objects in the solar system?

  A They caused craters to form on the surfaces of these objects.
  B They may have caused mass extinctions on Earth.
  C They caused much rock and other debris to be thrown into the air around the impact point.
  D all of the above

46. Astronomers have determined that there are nearly 150 planets beyond our solar system. They have determined this by

  A observing the planets using Earth-based telescopes.
  B observing stars exploding in supernovae.
  C measuring changes in stars' Doppler shifts.
  D all of the above

Directions: *Use the diagram below to answer Questions 47.*

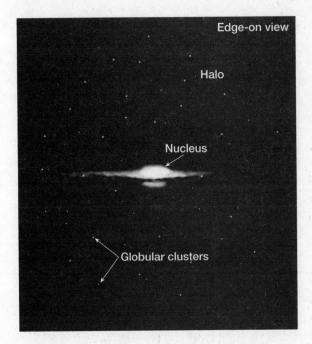

47. This image shows an edge view of the Milky Way Galaxy. Our solar system is located

  A in the halo of the galaxy.
  B close to the nucleus of the galaxy.
  C roughly midway along one of the galaxy's spiral arms.
  D near a globular cluster.

GO ON

Practice Test 2 (continued)

48. What type of matter composes much of the visible universe?

A galaxies
B dark matter
C black holes
D supernovae

49. Elements with an atomic number greater than that of lithium formed as the result of

A nuclear fission in laboratories.
B nuclear fusion in stars.
C chemosynthesis.
D photosynthesis.

50. What determines the stage a star is in at any time in its life cycle?

A gravity pushing outward on the star
B its temperature
C gravity and fusion
D energy from fusion pushing in on the star

51. By measuring the red shift of galaxies, astronomers have found that galaxies are moving away from Earth at different velocities. These observations are evidence that the universe is

A contracting.
B expanding.
C moving toward the blue end of the electromagnetic spectrum.
D all of the above

STOP

SAT II PRACTICE TEST

Directions: *Each of the following questions or incomplete statements is followed by five suggested answers or completions. Select the one that is best in each case.*

1. The portion of Earth that includes the oceans is called the

    (A) atmosphere.
    (B) biosphere.
    (C) geosphere.
    (D) hydrosphere.
    (E) troposphere.

2. The smallest particle of matter that still contains the characteristics of an element is a(n)

    (A) atom.
    (B) compound.
    (C) electron.
    (D) neutron.
    (E) proton.

3. Atoms that lose or accept electrons form a(n)

    (A) atomic bond.
    (B) covalent bond.
    (C) hydrogen bond.
    (D) ionic bond.
    (E) metallic bond.

Questions 4, 5, and 6
   I. Igneous rocks
  II. Metamorphic rocks
 III. Sedimentary rocks

4. These rocks are classified by texture and composition.

    (A) I
    (B) II
    (C) III
    (D) I and II
    (E) II and III

5. Pressure is partly responsible for forming these rocks.

    (A) I
    (B) II
    (C) III
    (D) I and II
    (E) II and III

6. These rocks are classified into granitic, andesitic, basaltic, and ultramafic.

    (A) I
    (B) II
    (C) III
    (D) I and II
    (E) II and III

SAT II Practice Test

GO ON

SAT II PRACTICE TEST (continued)

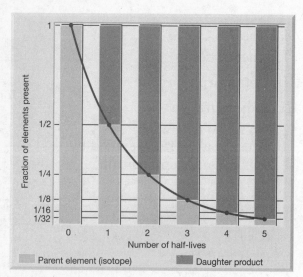

7. The information on the graph could be used by geologists in determining

  (A) the age of a living organism.
  (B) the absolute age of a rock.
  (C) the classification of index fossils.
  (D) the rate of evolution.
  (E) the relative age of a rock.

8. After three half-lives what percentage of daughter element remains?

  (A) 8%
  (B) 12.5%
  (C) 33%
  (D) 50%
  (E) 87.5%

9. A major force for chemical weathering is

  (A) frost wedging.
  (B) unloading.
  (C) water.
  (D) biological activity.
  (E) All of the above contribute to chemical weathering.

10. An oxbow lake forms from a(n)

  (A) meander.   (D) delta.
  (B) floodplain.   (E) tributary.
  (C) levee.

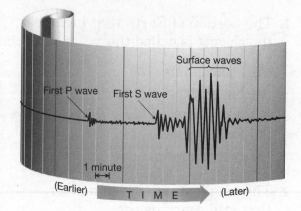

Questions 11 and 12

11. How much time passes between the start of the first P wave and the start of the first S wave?

  (A) 1 minute
  (B) 2 minutes
  (C) 3 minutes
  (D) 4 minutes
  (E) 5 minutes

12. Which portion of the seismograph records the arrival of seismic waves that compress and expand rocks as the waves travel through the ground?

  (A) The first P wave
  (B) The first S wave
  (C) The time difference between the waves
  (D) The surface waves
  (E) All of the measured waves

SAT Practice Test

SAT II PRACTICE TEST *(continued)*

13. The type of mass movement in which a block of material moves slowly along a curved surface is called

   (A) creep.
   (B) a mudflow.
   (C) a slump.
   (D) a rockslide.
   (E) an earthflow.

14. An area that has karst topography has largely been shaped by

   (A) mechanical weathering.
   (B) lava flows.
   (C) groundwater erosion.
   (D) glacial erosion.
   (E) stream erosion.

15. Which of the following features is not formed in front of a glacier?

   (A) cirque
   (B) drumlin
   (C) ground moraine
   (D) end moraine
   (E) kettle lake

16. Which of the following is a result of wind erosion or deposition?

   (A) loess
   (B) sand dune
   (C) desert pavement
   (D) deflation
   (E) All of the above are caused by wind.

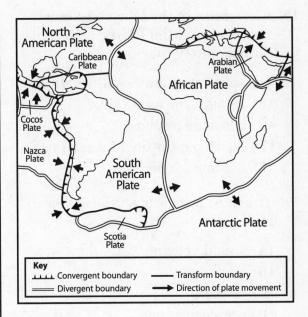

Question 17

17. According to the map above, the African plate and the South American plate are

   (A) subducting beneath a trench.
   (B) sliding past each other along a transform boundary.
   (C) moving apart along a divergent boundary.
   (D) two plates that are not in motion.
   (E) moving together along a convergent boundary.

GO ON

18. As a result of the long subduction zones around the Pacific plate, this plate is likely to

    (A) split into many smaller plates.

    (B) remain the same size.

    (C) become smaller.

    (D) develop a continental landmass.

    (E) become larger.

19. The most dangerous type of volcano is a

    (A) shield volcano.

    (B) cinder cone.

    (C) caldera.

    (D) composite cone.

    (E) lava plateau.

20. What type of geologic feature or activity is responsible for the creation of the Hawaiian islands?

    (A) a mantle plume

    (B) a convergent plate boundary

    (C) a divergent plate boundary

    (D) a columnar rock

    (E) a batholith

Questions 21, 22, and 23

  I. Normal fault

 II. Reverse fault

III. Thrust fault

IV. Strike-slip fault

21. Which fault(s) is/are compressional in nature?

    (A) I

    (B) II

    (C) III

    (D) IV

    (E) II and III

22. Which fault(s) is/are horizontal in nature?

    (A) I

    (B) II

    (C) III

    (D) IV

    (E) II and III

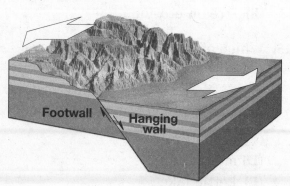

23. Which type of fault is shown above?

    (A) I

    (B) II

    (C) III

    (D) IV

    (E) This is not a fault.

GO ON

SAT II PRACTICE TEST (continued)

24. What usually occurs where two oceanic plates converge?

   (A) A continental volcanic arc forms.
   (B) A volcanic mountain forms.
   (C) An island arc forms.
   (D) An accretionary wedge forms.
   (E) A valley forms.

25. Which of the following provides indirect evidence of the behavior of an extinct organism?

   (A) a mold
   (B) a cast
   (C) a trace fossil
   (D) a carbonization
   (E) a petrified fossil

26. Which of the following ages is the earliest?

   (A) Age of Reptiles
   (B) Age of Amphibians
   (C) Age of Fishes
   (D) Age of Invertebrates
   (E) Age of Mammals

27. Which of the following periods includes the present time?

   (A) Tertiary Period
   (B) Quaternary Period
   (C) Cretaceous Period
   (D) Permian Period
   (E) Pennsylvanian Period

28. The deepest parts of the ocean are made up of

   (A) deep-ocean trenches.
   (B) abyssal plains.
   (C) hydrothermal vents.
   (D) seamounts.
   (E) guyots.

29. The factors that affect seawater density are

   (A) temperature and depth.
   (B) depth and location.
   (C) biomass content and salinity.
   (D) salinity and temperature.
   (E) location and biomass content.

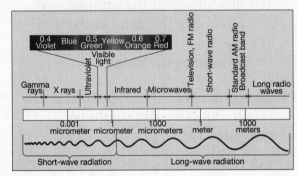

Questions 30 and 31

30. Which type of radiation has the longest wavelength?

   (A) gamma rays
   (B) visible light
   (C) ultraviolet waves
   (D) microwaves
   (E) infrared

SAT II PRACTICE TEST (continued)

31. Which type of radiation travels the fastest?

(A) gamma rays
(B) visible light
(C) long radio waves
(D) microwaves
(E) They all travel the same speed.

32. The Coriolis effect describes

(A) how the moon affects tidal patterns.
(B) how Earth's rotation affects moving objects.
(C) how temperature changes create pressure systems.
(D) how gases in the atmosphere affect Earth's temperature.
(E) how pressure and heat create metamorphic rocks.

33. An air mass that comes in from the north along a coast would be classified as

(A) continental polar.
(B) humid continental.
(C) maritime polar.
(D) maritime tropical.
(E) continental tropical.

34. Which of the following regions would most likely have a climate with warm temperatures year round?

(A) a region at sea level near the equator
(B) a region with an elevation above 2000 m
(C) a region near the center of a continent
(D) a region covered with dense forest
(E) a region at 40°N on the windward side of a mountain range.

35. Warm weather occurs during summer because

(A) Earth is closest to the sun.
(B) Earth is rotating at the slowest rate.
(C) Earth has less precipitation and cloud cover.
(D) Earth has a higher concentration of greenhouse gases.
(E) Earth is tilted toward the sun.

GO ON

SAT II PRACTICE TEST (continued)

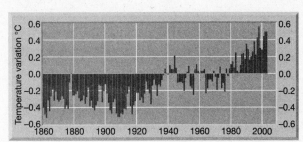

The figure above shows changes in Earth's average surface temperature.

36. According to the figure, which year had the highest average surface temperature on record?

(A) 2003
(B) 1998
(C) 1985
(D) 1909
(E) 1863

37. What do scientists think may have caused the global warming trend?

(A) A decrease in plant life
(B) An increase in greenhouse gases in the atmosphere
(C) A change in Earth's rotational axis
(D) An increase in acid rain
(E) A decrease in the ozone layer

38. During a total eclipse of the moon,

(A) Earth is completely in the penumbra.
(B) Earth is completely in the umbra.
(C) the moon is completely in the penumbra.
(D) the moon is completely in the umbra.
(E) Earth and moon are on opposite sides of the sun.

39. Which of the following planets does not fit easily into either the terrestrial or Jovian planet categories?

(A) Earth
(B) Uranus
(C) Pluto
(D) Mercury
(E) Mars

40. Most of the sunlight emitted from the sun comes from the

(A) photosphere.
(B) corona.
(C) chromosphere.
(D) core.
(E) prominence.

STOP

ACT PRACTICE TEST

Earth Science Test

DIRECTIONS: The passages below are each followed by several questions. After reading a passage, choose the best answer to each question. You may refer to the passages as often as necessary.

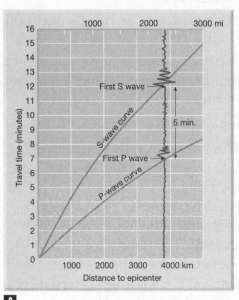

A

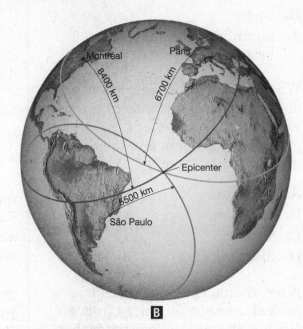

B

Passage I

A travel-time graph is used to determine the distance to the epicenter of an earthquake. The difference in arrival times of the first P wave and the first S wave in the graph is 5 minutes. So the epicenter is roughly 3800 kilometers away. The epicenter is located using the distance obtained from three seismic stations. The location in which the circles intersect is the epicenter.

1. According to the chart and illustration, what kind of data is needed to find the epicenter of an earthquake?

   A. wave magnitudes of both P waves and S waves

   B. distance between seismic wave occurrences

   C. time between P wave and S wave arrival

   D. intersection of the P wave and S waves

2. How many locations would be possible for an epicenter if only two seismic stations took measurements?

   F. one

   G. two

   H. three

   J. an unlimited number of locations

3. What would be the approximate distance from the Montreal seismic station to the epicenter if a P wave arrived at 01:36 pm and the S wave arrived at 01:40 pm?

   A. 1000 km

   B. 1500 km

   C. 2500 km

   D. 3200 km

4. What should the difference in arrival times be for waves from an earthquake with an epicenter that was approximately 1800 miles away?

   F. 2 minutes 30 seconds

   G. 3 minutes

   H. 4 minutes

   J. 4 minutes 30 seconds

Passage II

About 65 million years ago more than half of all plant and animal species died out in a mass extinction. This time marks the end of an era in which dinosaurs and other reptiles dominated the landscape.

The extinction of the dinosaurs is generally attributed to the group's inability to adapt to some radical change in the environment. What event could have caused the rapid extinction?

Hypothesis A

The most strongly supported hypothesis states that about 65 million years ago a large meteorite collided with Earth. The speed of the meteorite impact was believed to be 70,000 kilometers per hour. The force of the impact vaporized the meteorite and trillions of tons of Earth's crust. Huge quantities of dust and other debris were blasted high into the atmosphere. The encircling dust greatly restricted the sunlight reaching Earth's surface for months. Without sunlight for photosynthesis, delicate food chains collapsed. By the time the sunlight returned, more than half the species on Earth had become extinct.

There is some evidence to support the theory. A thin layer of sediment nearly 1 centimeter thick has been discovered worldwide. This sediment contains a high level of the element iridium, which is rare in Earth's crust but often found in meteorites.

GO ON

ACT PRACTICE TEST *(continued)*

Hypothesis B

Some scientists disagree with the impact hypothesis. These scientists suggest that huge volcanic eruptions led to the breakdown in the food chain. They cite enormous outpourings of lava in northern India about 65 million years ago as support for their thesis. These scientists dispute the age of the crater in Mexico that meteorite theorists believe was the impact site. They believe that these volcanic eruptions released the iridium onto the surface and flooded the atmosphere with carbon dioxide, which caused the dramatic environmental changes.

5. According to Passage II, what event do the majority of scientists believe caused the dinosaurs to become extinct?

   A. A meteorite hit Earth, raising large levels of dust that blocked the sun and created conditions that made it difficult for plants to grow.
   B. A meteorite hit Earth, creating a large crater and scattering debris that made it difficult for most life forms to breathe.
   C. Large-scale volcanic eruptions and a catastrophic event such as a meteorite impact combined to create a break-down in the food chain.
   D. Increased levels of iridium from a meteorite impact or volcanic eruption caused disruptions in the environment that led to mass extinctions.

6. What kind of evidence do opposing scientists use to dispute the meteorite impact theory?

   F. They believe that iridium comes from volcanoes, not meteorites.
   G. They believe that the layer of iridium dust is not consistent world-wide.
   H. They believe that a meteorite could not have created enough damage to cause extinctions.
   J. They do not believe that the age of the impact crater is consistent with the extinctions.

7. Which of the following statements is NOT a belief held by all scientists?

   A. A meteorite crashed into Earth 65 million years ago.
   B. A mass extinction took place 65 million years ago.
   C. A layer of iridium settled on Earth's surface 65 million years ago.
   D. Massive volcanic eruptions took place in India 65 million years ago.

8. Which piece of evidence is claimed as a part of both theories?

   F. huge quantities of dust found in the atmosphere
   G. a layer of iridium in the rock layer
   H. increased carbon dioxide levels in Earth's history
   J. a sudden decline in plant fossils

ACT PRACTICE TEST (continued)

9. What key element is indisputable for both teams of scientists in connection to the mass extinction?

   A. increased levels of carbon dioxide
   B. an interruption in the food chain
   C. a dramatic environmental change
   D. decreased levels of sunlight

10. What fact can you infer from the volcanic-activity theory?

   F. Iridium is also found beneath Earth's crust.
   G. Volcanic activity has caused other extinctions.
   H. Photosynthesis is not dependent on carbon dioxide.
   J. Dinosaurs were mostly plant-eaters.

Passage III

Relative humidity is a measurement used to describe water vapor in the air. In general, it expresses how close the air is to saturation. An investigation was conducted using a psychrometer to determine the relative humidity of air.

Part A. Calculating Relative Humidity from Water Vapor Content.

Relative humidity is the ratio of the air's water vapor content to its water vapor capacity at a given temperature. Relative humidity is expressed as a percent:

Relative humidity (%) = (Water vapor content/Water vapor capacity) × 100.

At 25°C, the water vapor capacity is 20 g/kg. The first part of the investigation involved taking data from three locations at 25°C and calculating the relative humidity.

Relative Humidity Determination Based on Water Vapor Content

Air Temperature (C)	Water Vapor Content (g/kg)	Water Vapor Capacity (g/kg)	Relative Humidity (%)
25	5	20	25
25	12		
25	18		

Part B. Determining Relative Humidity Using a Psychrometer.

A psychrometer consists of two thermometers. The wet-bulb thermometer has a cloth wick that is wet with water and spun for about 1 minute. Relative humidity is determined by the difference in temperature reading between the dry-bulb temperature and the wet-bulb temperature, and using Data Table 2. For example, suppose a dry-bulb temperature is measured as 20°C and a wet-bulb temperature is 14°C. The relative humidity would be 51 percent.

Data Table 2 Relative Humidity (percent)

Dry-bulb Temperature (C)	Depression of Wet-bulb Temperature (Dry-bulb Temperature − Wet-bulb Temperature = Depression of the Wet Bulb)																					
	1	2	3	4	5	6	7	8	9	10	11	12	13	14	15	16	17	18	19	20	21	22
−20	28																					
−18	40																					
−16	48	0																				
−14	55	11																				
−12	61	23																				
−10	66	33	0																			
−8	71	41	13																			
−6	73	48	20	0																		
−4	77	54	43	11																		
−2	79	58	37	20	1																	
0	81	63	45	28	11																	
2	83	67	51	36	20	6																
4	85	70	56	42	27	14																
6	86	72	59	46	35	22	10	0														
8	87	74	62	51	39	28	17	6														
10	88	76	65	54	43	33	24	13	4													
12	88	78	67	57	48	38	28	19	10	2												
14	89	79	69	60	50	41	33	25	16	8	1											
16	90	80	71	62	54	45	37	29	21	14	7	1										
18	91	81	72	64	56	48	40	33	26	19	12	6	0									
20	91	82	74	66	58	51	44	36	30	23	17	11	5	0								
22	92	83	75	68	60	53	46	40	33	27	21	15	10	4	0							
24	92	84	76	69	62	55	49	42	36	30	25	20	14	9	4	0						
26	92	85	77	70	64	57	51	45	39	34	28	23	18	13	9	5						
28	93	86	78	71	65	59	53	47	42	36	31	26	22	18	14	9	5	2				
30	93	86	79	72	66	61	55	49	44	39	34	29	25	20	16	12	8	4				
32	93	86	80	73	68	62	56	51	46	41	36	32	27	22	19	14	11	8	4			
34	93	86	81	74	69	63	58	52	48	43	38	34	30	26	22	18	14	11	8	5		
36	94	87	81	75	69	64	59	54	50	44	40	36	32	28	24	21	17	13	10	7	4	
38	94	87	82	76	70	66	60	55	51	46	42	38	34	30	26	23	20	16	13	10	7	5
40	94	89	82	76	71	67	61	57	52	48	44	40	36	33	29	25	22	19	16	13	10	7

Relative Humidity Values

ACT Practice Test

GO ON

ACT PRACTICE TEST (continued)

11. Follow the procedure in Passage III for calculating relative humidity using the water vapor content. What would you expect to fill in as the relative humidity when the air temperature is 25°C and the water vapor content is 18 g/kg?

    A. 25%
    B. 40%
    C. 60%
    D. 90%

12. What information must already be known before determining relative humidity based on the water vapor content?

    F. the water vapor content
    G. the water vapor temperature
    H. the water vapor capacity
    J. the water vapor depression

13. Which information is NOT needed to calculate relative humidity using the psychrometer?

    A. dry bulb temperature
    B. wet bulb temperature
    C. air pressure
    D. relative humidity values

14. Why were two temperature measurements needed to find the relative humidity in Part B of Passage III?

    F. to reduce the possibility of error
    G. to find an average
    H. to find a difference
    J. to create a range

15. Why is the relative humidity expressed as a percentage?

    A. The relative humidity is a measure of how much of the total volume of air is filled with water vapor.
    B. The relative humidity compares one temperature reading with another in terms of the percentage.
    C. The relative humidity is not an absolute measurement using any standard scale and is instead comparative.
    D. The relative humidity requires additional data to be used with the percentage in order to be applicable.

GO ON

ACT PRACTICE TEST (continued)

Ocean Surface Currents

A world map showing ocean surface currents with warm (solid arrows) and cold (dashed arrows) currents labeled, including: Labrador C., E. Greenland C., Norwegian C., Alaskan C., N. Pacific C., California C., Gulf Stream, N. Atlantic C., Canary C., Oyashio C., Kuroshio C., North Pacific Gyre, North Atlantic Gyre, N. Equatorial C., Somali C., N. Equatorial C., S. Equatorial C., S. Equatorial C., S. Equatorial C., Peru C., Brazil C., Benguela C., Agulhas C., Indian Ocean Gyre, W. Australian C., Leeuwin C., E. Australian C., South Pacific Gyre, South Atlantic Gyre, West Wind Drift, East Wind Drift.

Passage IV

Huge, circular-moving current systems dominate the surfaces of the oceans. These large whirls of water within an ocean basin are called gyres. The ocean's circulation is organized into five major gyres, or circular current systems. The West Wind Drift flows around the continent of Antarctica. Use the map of Ocean Surface Currents to answer the questions below.

16. What type of currents make up the South Atlantic Gyre?

   F. warm currents
   G. cold currents
   H. warm and cold currents
   J. clockwise currents

17. What characteristic contrasts the gyres in the Northern Hemisphere with the gyres in the Southern hemisphere?

   A. warm versus cold currents
   B. circular versus straight systems
   C. clockwise versus counter clockwise rotation
   D. equatorial versus non-equatorial currents

18. Which gyre does not include an equatorial current?

   F. the South Pacific Gyre
   G. the South Atlantic Gyre
   H. the Indian Ocean Gyre
   J. They all include an equatorial current.

ACT Practice Test

19. Which ocean current completely circles the Earth without interruption?

    A. West Wind Drift

    B. Gulf Stream

    C. North Equatorial Current

    D. South Equatorial Current

20. Which of the following currents is *not* part of the Indian Ocean gyre?

    F. West Australian Current

    G. Leeuwin Current

    H. South Equatorial Current

    J. Agulhas Current

Passage V

Communities are constantly looking for alternate ways to get the energy needed to serve their growing populations. When creating a power plant to supply a community without using fossil fuels, several options are available for consideration. Some of the most popular choices are between solar energy, nuclear energy, and hydroelectric power.

Solar Energy

Solar energy is the direct use of the sun's rays to supply heat or electricity. Solar energy has two advantages: the "fuel" is free, and it is non-polluting. Active solar collectors are used to heat water for domestic and commercial needs. For example, solar collectors provide hot water for more than 80 percent of Israel's homes. A solar collection facility heats water in pressurized panels. The superheated water is then transferred to turbines, which turn electrical generators.

There are a few drawbacks to solar energy. While the energy collected is free, the necessary equipment and installation is not. A supplemental heating unit is also needed when there is less solar energy, such as on cloudy days or in the winter. Solar energy is economical in some areas of the United States and will become even more cost effective as the prices of other fuels increase.

Nuclear Energy

Nuclear power meets about 7 percent of the energy demand of the United States. The fuel for nuclear plants comes from radioactive materials that release energy through nuclear fission. In a nuclear power plant the fission reaction is controlled by moving neutron-absorbing rods into or out of the nuclear reactor. The result is a controlled nuclear chain reaction that releases great amounts of heat. The energy drives steam turbines that turn electrical generators.

At one time, energy experts thought nuclear power would be the cheap, clean energy source that would replace fossil fuels. But several obstacles have slowed its development. First, the cost of building safe nuclear facilities has increased. Second, there are hazards associated with the disposal of nuclear wastes. Third, there is concern over the possibility of a serious accident that could cause radioactive materials to escape.

Hydroelectric Power

Hydroelectric power uses falling water to turn turbines and produce electricity. In the United States, hydroelectric

ACT PRACTICE TEST (continued)

power plants produce about 5 percent of the country's electricity. Large dams are responsible for creating most of it by allowing a controlled flow of water.

Although water power is a renewable resource, hydroelectric dams have finite lifetimes. Rivers deposit sediment behind the dam, eventually filling the reservoir. This process takes 50 to 300 years and when it is filled, the dam can no longer produce power. The availability of suitable sites is an important limiting factor in the development of hydroelectric power plants. A good site must provide a significant height for the water to fall. Most of the best sites within the United States have already been developed.

21. Which of the following is **not** true of solar energy as a source for power generation?

   A. Solar energy requires sunny weather.

   B. On cloudy days, a supplemental heating unit may be needed.

   C. Solar energy is "free."

   D. Solar collectors are rarely used to heat water.

22. One main advantage of a hydroelectric power plant, as compared with a nuclear power plant, is that it

   F. uses a renewable energy source.

   G. has an unlimited lifetime.

   H. costs very little.

   J. does not require a specific type of site.

23. Which of the following is a major disadvantage of hydroelectric power?

   A. Hydroelectric power is non-renewable.

   B. Hydroelectric power is limited to sites that provide enough height for water to fall.

   C. Hydroelectric power causes air and water pollution.

   D. Large dams are too expensive to build.

24. Which of the following is common to all three alternative energy sources in generating large amounts of electricity for a community?

   F. All three sources involve generating some waste products.

   G. All three are unaffected by local climate conditions.

   H. All three sources involve using water or steam to turn turbines.

   J. All three sources are inadequate for supplying large amounts of power.

ACT PRACTICE TEST *(continued)*

25. The lifetime of a hydroelectric power plant may be limited by

  A. turbines wearing out.
  B. erosion of the cement in the dam.
  C. buildup of sediment in the reservoir behind the dam.
  D. changes in the price of electricity.

Passage VI

Most soils contain particles of different sizes. Soil texture refers to the proportions of different particle sizes. To classify soil texture, the U.S. Department of Agriculture has established categories based on the percentages of clay, silt, and sand in soil. The diagram shows how the percentages differ for each category. For example, point A represents a soil that is 40 percent clay, 10 percent silt, and 50 percent sand.

Texture strongly influences a soil's ability to support plant life. Sandy soils may drain quickly, while clay-rich soils drain very slowly. Plant roots often have difficulty penetrating soils that contain a high percentage of clay and silt. Loam soils are usually best for plant growth. They retain water better and store more nutrients than do soils composed mainly of clay or sand.

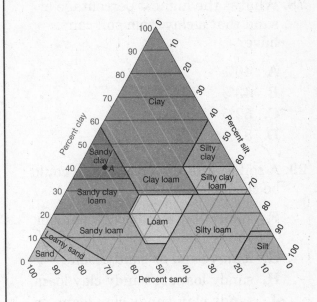

26. Based on the diagram, which of the following best describes composition of *loam*?

  A. 40% silt, 40% sand, 20% clay
  B. 70% silt, 30% sand
  C. 20% clay, 70% sand, 10% silt
  D. 40% clay, 60% silt

27. Which type of soil contains a higher percentage of silt?

  F. silty loam
  G. silty clay loam
  H. loam
  J. silty clay

GO ON

ACT PRACTICE TEST *(continued)*

28. What is the highest percentage of sand that a clay loam soil can have?

    A. 40%
    B. 43%
    C. 52%
    D. 84%

29. A soil that is 70 percent sand could be classified as

    F. sandy clay, sandy clay loam, or sandy loam.
    G. loamy sand or sandy loam.
    H. sandy loam or sandy clay loam.
    J. sandy clay, sandy clay loam, or loam.

30. Which type of soil would be best to use for gardening where rich soil with good drainage is important?

    F. silty clay loam
    G. sandy loam
    H. sandy clay loam
    J. sandy clay

31. Which term describes a soil that is 60 percent silt, 30 percent clay, and 10 percent sand?

    A. silty clay
    B. sandy clay loam
    C. silty loam
    D. silty clay loam

Passage VII

Ocean water temperatures vary from equator to pole and change with depth. Temperature, like salinity, affects the density of seawater. However, the density of seawater is more sensitive to temperature fluctuations than salinity.

An experiment was set up to determine the effects of temperature on water density. The procedure is outlined below.

Part A

1. Mix cold tap water with ice cubes in a beaker. Stir until the water and ice are well mixed. Fill a graduated cylinder with 100 mL of cold water from the beaker. Make sure no ice gets into the graduated cylinder.

2. Put 2 to 3 drops of dye in a test tube and fill it half full of hot tap water. Pour the contents of the test tube into the graduated cylinder and record observations.

<u>Scientist's observation: The hot water stayed near the surface in the graduated cylinder.</u>

3. Add a test tube full of cold tap water to a beaker. Mix in 2 to 3 drops of dye and a handful of ice to the beaker. Stir the solution thoroughly. Fill the test tube half full of this solution. Do not allow any ice into the test tube.

4. Fill a second graduated cylinder with 100 mL of hot tap water.

5. Pour the test tube of cold liquid slowly into the cylinder of hot water. Record your observations.

ACT PRACTICE TEST (continued)

Scientist's observation: The cold water sank beneath the warmer water in the graduated cylinder.

Part B

Idealized Ocean Surface Water Temperatures and Densities at Various Latitudes		
Latitude	Surface Temperature (C)	Surface Density (g/cm³)
60N	5	1.0258
40	13	1.0259
20	24	1.0237
0	27	1.0238
20	24	1.0241
40	15	1.0261
60S	2	1.0272

32. What can you infer from the first observation made by the scientist?

F. The hot water and the cold water were similar in density.

G. The cold water was less dense than the hot water.

H. The hot water had a lower density than the cold water.

J. No inference about density can be drawn.

33. Which purpose does the dye serve in this experiment?

A. It acts as a control.

B. It acts as an identifier.

C. It acts as a measurement tool.

D. It acts as a timer.

34. Which statement best describes the relationship shown by the results?

F. Increased temperature causes an increase in density.

G. Increased temperature causes a decrease in density.

H. Increased density causes an increase in temperature.

J. Increased density causes a decrease in temperature.

35. Study the table in Part B. The data in the table show that

A. warmer waters tend to collect at higher latitudes.

B. water near the equator is less dense than other areas.

C. the least dense water is found at 40°N and 40°S latitude.

D. water at higher latitudes becomes less dense.

36. According to the table, the surface density of ocean water north of the equator

F. stays the same as latitude increases.

G. increases steadily as latitude increases.

H. decreases slightly, increases, and then decreases slightly at 60°N.

J. decreases steadily as latitude increases.

GO ON

37. Which statement best describes the general relationship between the latitude, temperature and density of ocean surface water?

A. As temperature decreases with latitude, density also increases.

B. Temperature increases with latitude, but density remains constant.

C. As temperature decreases with latitude, density generally increases.

D. There is no relationship between latitude, temperature, and density.

Passage VIII

Global warming is perhaps one of the most hotly debated environmental issues. Is the world getting warmer, and should society worry about it? Many scientists think that global warming is an important issue that may have devastating consequences for humanity. Other scientists think that the global warming issue is overblown and that there is very little need to worry. Below are two sides of the issue.

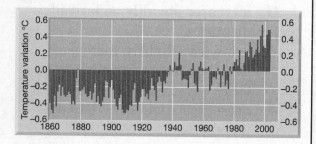

Opinion A

Global Warming is cause for alarm: As a result of increases in carbon dioxide levels, as well as other greenhouse gases, global temperatures have

increased. Scientists attribute the increase in carbon dioxide to human activity, especially the burning of fossil fuels. The figure above shows that during the twentieth century, Earth's average surface temperature increased about 0.6°C. Scientists predict that by the year 2100, temperatures will increase by 1.4°C to 5.8°C. Warmer temperatures increase evaporation rates. This, in turn, increases the amount of water vapor in the atmosphere. Water vapor is an even more powerful absorber of radiation emitted by Earth than carbon dioxide. Therefore, more water vapor in the air will magnify the effect of carbon dioxide and other gases.

Temperature increases will also melt sea ice and ice sheets, causing a global rise in sea level. This will lead to shoreline erosion and coastal flooding. Scientists also expect that weather patterns will change as a result of the projected global warming. Hurricanes will increase in number and intense heat waves and droughts will occur in some regions.

Opinion B

Global warming is not a threat: Some skeptics say the scientific models used to predict the climate do not deal with the planet's complex ecosystem. The atmosphere is too complex for computer models to predict successfully what Earth's climate will be like centuries into the future. If it could be done, scientists say, then global climate models should be able to predict changes a year into the future, which they cannot do.

ACT PRACTICE TEST *(continued)*

Although skeptics agree that the climate has changed recently, they believe that climate change is a natural phenomenon that does not pose a threat to humans. They point out that Earth has gone through many climate changes in its history that are unrelated to human activity. They also argue that the kind of data that are needed to show temperature trends has only been available for the last hundred years or so–too short a time period in which to create a reliable model.

Other scientists argue that even if global warming is occurring, the change in temperature is not enough to warrant such alarm. They point out that many parts of the world experience huge changes in climate regularly with no bad effects. They also argue that the warming trend will be offset by adjustments in Earth's climate system, such as the formation of more clouds. More clouds would reflect more solar radiation back into space and tend to reduce warming.

38. Which of the following states one criticism that skeptics have of the graph showing a global warming trend?

    F. The graph does not show a clear increase in temperatures.

    G. The graph does not include information from different parts of the world.

    H. The graph does not show a pattern or trend in the data.

    J. The graph does not include temperatures from a long enough period of time.

39. What do scientists who warn of global warming predict about the effects of increased evaporation?

    A. They believe that evaporation would cause temperatures to increase even more.

    B. They believe that evaporation would cause temperatures to cool slightly.

    C. They believe that evaporation would cause an increase in the amount of carbon dioxide in the atmosphere.

    D. They believe that evaporation would remove carbon dioxide from the air.

40. Which of the following is NOT an argument used by skeptics about global warming?

    F. Earth's temperature is not increasing any more than other times in history.

    G. Global warming does not cause problems for the environment.

    H. There are no data to indicate that the temperature of Earth is increasing.

    J. Earth's atmosphere responds to global warming to correct it.

Diagnostic Test A Report

National Science Education Standards	Test Items	Number Correct	Proficient? Yes or No	Student Edition Chapter/Lesson
Content Standard A: Science as Inquiry				
A-1. Abilities necessary to do scientific inquiry	7, 72, 74, 75, 140	☐ 5		activities, 1.1, 1.2, 1.3, 1.4, 1.5
A-2. Understandings about scientific inquiry	1, 2, 23, 49, 56, 58, 59, 72, 76, 77, 84, 110, 118	☐ 13		1.3, 1.5, 2.3, 8.2, 8.3, 8.4, 9.1, 9.4, 11.1, 12.3, 13.1, 14.1, 14.2, 19.1, 19.3, 22.1, 22.3, 23.2, 23.3, 23.4, 24.1, 25.1, 25.2, 25.3
Content Standard B: Physical Science				
B-1. Structure of atoms	9, 10	☐ 2		2.1, 4.2, 5.1, 24.3, 25.2
B-2. Structure and properties of matter	8, 12, 13, 14, 18, 19, 20, 89	☐ 8		2.1, 2.2, 2.3, 3.2, 7.1, 12.3, 18.8, 18.3
B-3. Chemical reactions	11, 21, 22, 63, 73, 87, 88, 100, 105, 109	☐ 10		2.1, 3.4, 4.1, 4.3, 5.2, 7.2, 14.2, 21.3, 25.2
B-4. Motion and forces	36, 38, 39, 40, 47, 48, 66, 67, 68, 99, 108, 112, 115, 138	☐ 14		16.2, 19.1, 19.2, 22.1, 22.3, 23.1, 25.2
B-5. Conservation of energy and increase in disorder	62, 78, 102, 103, 129	☐ 5		17.2, 17.3, 18.1, 18.2, 20.2, 24.3, 25.1
B-6. Interactions of energy and matter	44, 45, 46, 104, 106, 107, 111, 120, 121, 124, 137	☐ 11		8.1, 8.2, 8.3, 8.4, 9.4, 16.2, 16.3, 17.2, 24.1, 24.2, 24.3, 25.2
Content Standard C: Life Science				
C-1. The cell	79	☐ 1		15.3
C-3. Biological evolution	79, 80, 81	☐ 3		13.2, 13.3, 13.4
C-4. Interdependence of organisms	91, 92	☐ 2		1.2, 1.4, 4.1, 4.2, 4.3, 4.4, 5.2, 6.1, 15.2, 15.3, 16.1, 16.3, 17.1, 21.3

Name _____ Date _____ Class _____

National Science Education Standards	Test Items	Number Correct	Proficient? Yes or No	Student Edition Chapter/Lesson
C-5. Matter, energy, and organization in living systems	29, 93, 125	☐ 3		4.1, 15.1, 15.2, 15.3
C-6. Behavior of organisms	90	☐ 1		15.2
Content Standard D: Earth Science				
D-1. Energy in the earth system	16, 17, 32, 33, 37, 60, 61, 65, 69, 70, 85, 86, 94, 95, 96, 97, 98, 101, 113, 114, 116, 117, 119, 122, 123, 126, 127, 128	☐ 28		1.1, 1.2, 1.4, 3.1, 4.2, 4.3, 5.1, 6.1, 6.3, 9.2, 9.3, 9.4, 10.3, 13.2, 15.1, 16.1, 16.2, 16.3, 17.1, 17.2, 17.3, 18.2, 18.3, 19.1, 19.2, 19.3, 20.1, 21.1, 21.2, 21.3, 23.2, 24.3
D-2. Geochemical cycles	15	☐ 1		1.4, 2.2. 3.1, 3.3, 3.4, 4.1, 4.3, 5.1, 5.2, 6.1, 7.1, 7.2, 7.3, 8.4, 10.1, 10.2, 10.3, 12.2, 12.3, 14.2, 14.3, 14.4, 15.1, 16.1, 17.2, 18.1
D-3. Origin and evolution of the earth system	55, 133, 134, 135, 136, 139	☐ 6		1.1, 1.2, 1.4, 2.1, 3.3, 4.1, 7.1, 8.1, 8.2, 8.3, 9.1, 9.2, 9.3, 9.4, 10.1, 11.1, 11.2, 11.3, 12.1, 12.2, 12.3, 12.4, 13.1, 13.2, 13.3, 13.4, 16.3, 17.1, 21.3, 22.1, 22.2, 22.3, 23.1, 24.3
D-4. Origin and evolution of the universe	141, 142, 143	☐ 3		24.3, 25.1, 25.2, 25.3
Content Standard E: Science and Technology				
E-1. Abilities of technological design	54, 75	☐ 2		8.4
E-2. Understandings about science and technology	52, 53, 74, 82, 83	☐ 5		1.3, 4.1, 4.2, 6.2, 8.2, 8.3, 8.4, 9.1, 9.4, 14.1, 14.4, 22.1, 22.3, 23.2, 23.3, 23.4, 24.1, 24.2, 24.3, 25.3
Content Standard F: Science in Personal and Social Perspectives				
F-1. Personal and community health	6	☐ 1		1.4, 4.3
F-3. Natural resources	24, 25, 26, 27, 34, 42	☐ 6		1.4, 4.1, 4.2, 4.3, 4.4, 5.2, 6.3, 14.2, 14.4

Diagnostic Test A Report

Name _____ Date _____ Class _____

National Science Education Standards	Test Items	Number Correct	Proficient? Yes or No	Student Edition Chapter/Lesson
F-4. Environmental quality	30, 31	☐ 2		1.4, 4.1, 4.2, 4.3, 4.4, 5.1, 5.2, 6.3, 17.1
F-5. Natural and human-induced hazards	41, 43, 50, 51, 54, 64, 130	☐ 7		1.4, 4.1, 4.2, 4.3, 4.4, 5.1, 5.2, 5.3, 6.1, 6.2, 6.3, 7.2, 7.3, 8.1, 8.2, 8.3, 10.1, 20.1, 20.3, 21.3
F-6. Science and technology in local, national, and global challenges	28, 35	☐ 2		1.4, 4.1, 4.2, 4.3, 4.4, 5.2, 6.2, 6.3, 8.2, 8.3, 16.3, 20.3, 21.3
Content Standard G: History and Nature of Science				
G-1. Science as a human endeavor	3, 4, 5, 71, 72, 77, 140	☐ 7		8.3, 9.1, 9.2, 9.3, 9.4, 12.1, 12.2, 12.4, 13.2, 14.1, 14.2, 19.3, 22.1, 24.1, 24.2, 25.1
G-2. Nature of scientific knowledge	57, 58, 59	☐ 3		1.1, 1.5, 2.3, 5.3, 8.3, 9.1, 9.4, 10.2, 11.3, 12.1, 12.2, 12.4, 13.4, 22.1, 24.1, 25.2
G-3. Historical perspectives	56, 71, 131, 132	☐ 4		1.1, 1.2, 1.3, 1.5, 7.1, 9.1, 9.2, 9.3, 10.3, 11.3, 12.1, 12.2, 12.4, 16.2, 22.1, 24.1, 24.2, 24.3, 25.1, 25.2, 25.3

Student Comments: _____

_____

_____

_____

Parent Comments: _____

_____

_____

_____

Teacher Comments: _____

_____

_____

_____

Diagnostic Test A Report

Name _____ Date _____ Class _____

Diagnostic Test B Report

National Science Education Standards	Test Items	Number Correct	Proficient? Yes or No	Student Edition Chapter/Lesson
Content Standard A: Science as Inquiry				
A-1. Abilities necessary to do scientific inquiry	49	☐ 1		activities, 1.1, 1.2, 1.3, 1.4, 1.5
A-2. Understandings about scientific inquiry	3, 4, 10, 11, 36, 37, 50, 51, 52, 64, 69, 74, 76, 100, 107, 109, 115	☐ 17		1.3, 1.5, 2.3, 8.2, 8.3, 8.4, 9.1, 9.4, 11.1, 12.3, 13.1, 14.1, 14.2, 19.1, 19.3, 22.1, 22.3, 23.2, 23.3, 23.4, 24.1, 25.1, 25.2, 25.3
Content Standard B: Physical Science				
B-1. Structure of atoms	7	☐ 1		2.1, 4.2, 5.1, 24.3, 25.2
B-2. Structure and properties of matter	9, 12, 13, 14, 18, 20, 77	☐ 7		2.1, 2.2, 2.3, 3.2, 7.1, 12.3, 18.8, 18.3
B-3. Chemical reactions	8, 16, 19, 28, 39, 67, 80	☐ 7		2.1, 3.4, 4.1, 4.3, 5.2, 7.2, 14.2, 21.3, 25.2
B-4. Motion and forces	31, 32, 35, 59, 60, 61, 88, 89, 103	☐ 9		16.2, 19.1, 19.2, 22.1, 22.3, 23.1, 25.2
B-5. Conservation of energy and increase in disorder	34, 42, 87, 93, 94, 96, 98, 101	☐ 8		17.2, 17.3, 18.1, 18.2, 20.2, 24.3, 25.1
B-6. Interactions of energy and matter	38, 40, 43, 97, 102	☐ 4		8.1, 8.2, 8.3, 8.4, 9.4, 16.2, 16.3, 17.2, 24.1, 24.2, 24.3, 25.2
Content Standard C: Life Science				
C-2. Molecular basis of heredity	70	☐ 1		
C-3. Biological evolution	65, 66, 70, 71, 73	☐ 5		13.2, 13.3, 13.4
C-5. Matter, energy, and organization in living systems	72, 83, 84	☐ 3		4.1, 15.1, 15.2, 15.3

Diagnostic Test B Report

Name _____ Date _____ Class _____

National Science Education Standards	Test Items	Number Correct	Proficient? Yes or No	Student Edition Chapter/Lesson
C-6. Behavior of organisms	82	☐ 1		15.2
Content Standard D: Earth Science				
D-1. Energy in the earth system	5, 15, 17, 33, 41, 54, 55, 57, 58, 62, 63, 81, 85, 86, 91, 92, 95, 99, 104, 105, 106, 108, 110, 111, 112, 113, 114, 116, 117	☐ 29		1.1, 1.2, 1.4, 3.1, 4.2, 4.3, 5.1, 6.1, 6.3, 9.2, 9.3, 9.4, 10.3, 13.2, 15.1, 16.1, 16.2, 16.3, 17.1, 17.2, 17.3, 18.2, 18.3, 19.1, 19.2, 19.3, 20.1, 21.1, 21.2, 21.3, 23.2, 24.3
D-3. Origin and evolution of the earth system	1, 2, 48, 121, 122, 123, 124, 125, 126, 127, 134, 135	☐ 12		1.1, 1.2, 1.4, 2.1, 3.3, 4.1, 7.1, 8.1, 8.2, 8.3, 9.1, 9.2, 9.3, 9.4, 10.1, 11.1, 11.2, 11.3, 12.1, 12.2, 12.3, 12.4, 13.1, 13.2, 13.3, 13.4, 16.3, 17.1, 21.3, 22.1, 22.2, 22.3, 23.1, 24.3
D-4. Origin and evolution of the universe	128, 129, 130, 138, 139, 140, 141, 142	☐ 8		24.3, 25.1, 25.2, 25.3
Content Standard E: Science and Technology				
E-1. Abilities of technological design	46, 75, 131, 132, 133	☐ 5		8.4
E-2. Understandings about science and technology	49, 68, 136	☐ 3		1.3, 4.1, 4.2, 6.2, 8.2, 8.3, 8.4, 9.1, 9.4, 14.1, 14.4, 22.1, 22.3, 23.2, 23.3, 23.4, 24.1, 24.2, 24.3, 25.3
Content Standard F: Science in Personal and Social Perspectives				
F-1. Personal and community health	23, 24	☐ 2		1.4, 4.3
F-2. Population growth	119	☐ 1		1.4, 4.1, 4.2, 4.4
F-3. Natural resources	6, 21, 22, 25, 26, 29, 30, 78, 79	☐ 9		1.4, 4.1, 4.2, 4.3, 4.4, 5.2, 6.3, 14.2, 14.4
F-4. Environmental quality	27, 90	☐ 2		1.4, 4.1, 4.2, 4.3, 4.4, 5.1, 5.2, 6.3, 17.1

Diagnostic Test B Report

National Science Education Standards	Test Items	Number Correct	Proficient? Yes or No	Student Edition Chapter/Lesson
F-5. Natural and human-induced hazards	44, 45, 47, 56, 118, 119	☐ 6		1.4, 4.1, 4.2, 4.3, 4.4, 5.1, 5.2, 5.3, 6.1, 6.2, 6.3, 7.2, 7.3, 8.1, 8.2, 8.3, 10.1, 20.1, 20.3, 21.3
F-6. Science and technology in local, national, and global challenges	23, 24, 119	☐ 3		1.4, 4.1, 4.2, 4.3, 4.4, 5.2, 6.2, 6.3, 8.2, 8.3, 16.3, 20.3, 21.3
Content Standard G: History and Nature of Science				
G-1. Science as a human endeavor	4, 49, 64, 69, 100, 137	☐ 6		8.3, 9.1, 9.2, 9.3, 9.4, 12.1, 12.2, 12.4, 13.2, 14.1, 14.2, 19.3, 22.1, 24.1, 24.2, 25.1
G-2. Nature of scientific knowledge	50, 52, 53, 115, 137	☐ 5		1.1, 1.5, 2.3, 5.3, 8.3, 9.1, 9.4, 10.2, 11.3, 12.1, 12.2, 12.4, 13.4, 22.1, 24.1, 25.2
G-3. Historical perspectives	50, 120	☐ 2		1.1, 1.2, 1.3, 1.5, 7.1, 9.1, 9.2, 9.3, 10.3, 11.3, 12.1, 12.2, 12.4, 16.2, 22.1, 24.1, 24.2, 24.3, 25.1, 25.2, 25.3

Student Comments: _____

_____

_____

_____

Parent Comments: _____

_____

_____

_____

Teacher Comments: _____

_____

_____

_____

Name _____ Date _____ Class _____

Benchmark Test 1 Report

National Science Education Standards	Test Items	Number Correct	Proficient? Yes or No	Student Edition Chapter/Lesson
Content Standard A: Science as Inquiry				
A-1. Abilities necessary to do scientific inquiry	5, 9, 13	☐ 3		activities, 1.1, 1.2, 1.3, 1.4, 1.5
A-2. Understandings about scientific inquiry	1, 3, 4, 5, 6, 7, 8, 9, 21, 23, 33, 37, 38, 43, 68	☐ 15		1.3, 1.5, 2.3, 8.2, 8.3, 8.4, 9.1, 9.4, 11.1, 12.3, 13.1, 14.1, 14.2, 19.1, 19.3, 22.1, 22.3, 23.2, 23.3, 23.4, 24.1, 25.1, 25.2, 25.3
Content Standard B: Physical Science				
B-1. Structure of atoms	15, 16	☐ 2		2.1, 4.2, 5.1, 24.3, 25.2
B-2. Structure and properties of matter	14, 19, 22, 24, 25, 26, 27, 29, 30	☐ 9		2.1, 2.2, 2.3, 3.2, 7.1, 12.3, 18.8, 18.3
B-3. Chemical reactions	17, 18, 20, 34, 35, 41, 60	☐ 7		2.1, 3.4, 4.1, 4.3, 5.2, 7.2, 14.2, 21.3, 25.2
B-4. Motion and forces	66, 67	☐ 2		16.2, 19.1, 19.2, 22.1, 22.3, 23.1, 25.2
B-5. Conservation of energy and increase in disorder	40	☐ 1		17.2, 17.3, 18.1, 18.2, 20.2, 24.3, 25.1
B-6. Interactions of energy and matter	59	☐ 1		8.1, 8.2, 8.3, 8.4, 9.4, 16.2, 16.3, 17.2, 24.1, 24.2, 24.3, 25.2
Content Standard C: Life Science				
Content Standard D: Earth Science			•	
D-1. Energy in the earth system	10, 31, 32, 36, 39, 42, 61	☐ 7		1.1, 1.2, 1.4, 3.1, 4.2, 4.3, 5.1, 6.1, 6.3, 9.2, 9.3, 9.4, 10.3, 13.2, 15.1, 16.1, 16.2, 16.3, 17.1, 17.2, 17.3, 18.2, 18.3, 19.1, 19.2, 19.3, 20.1, 21.1, 21.2, 21.3, 23.2, 24.3

Benchmark Test 1 Report

National Science Education Standards	Test Items	Number Correct	Proficient? Yes or No	Student Edition Chapter/Lesson
D-2. Geochemical cycles	28, 54	2		1.4, 2.2. 3.1, 3.3, 3.4, 4.1, 4.3, 5.1, 5.2, 6.1, 7.1, 7.2, 7.3, 8.4, 10.1, 10.2, 10.3, 12.2, 12.3, 14.2, 14.3, 14.4, 15.1, 16.1, 17.2, 18.1
D-3. Origin and evolution of the earth system	2	1		1.1, 1.2, 1.4, 2.1, 3.3, 4.1, 7.1, 8.1, 8.2, 8.3, 9.1, 9.2, 9.3, 9.4, 10.1, 11.1, 11.2, 11.3, 12.1, 12.2, 12.3, 12.4, 13.1, 13.2, 13.3, 13.4, 16.3, 17.1, 21.3, 22.1, 22.2, 22.3, 23.1, 24.3
Content Standard E: Science and Technology				
E-1. Abilities of technological design	50	1		8.4
E-2. Understandings about science and technology	50, 51	2		1.3, 4.1, 4.2, 6.2, 8.2, 8.3, 8.4, 9.1, 9.4, 14.1, 14.4, 22.1, 22.3, 23.2, 23.3, 23.4, 24.1, 24.2, 24.3, 25.3
Content Standard F: Science in Personal and Social Perspectives				
F-1. Personal and community health	11, 49, 65	3		1.4, 4.3
F-3. Natural resources	12, 44, 45, 47, 48, 52, 53, 55, 58, 62, 63, 64	12		1.4, 4.1, 4.2, 4.3, 4.4, 5.2, 6.3, 14.2, 14.4
F-4. Environmental quality	11, 54, 56, 57, 58	5		1.4, 4.1, 4.2, 4.3, 4.4, 5.1, 5.2, 6.3, 17.1
F-5. Natural and human-induced hazards	11, 65	2		1.4, 4.1, 4.2, 4.3, 4.4, 5.1, 5.2, 5.3, 6.1, 6.2, 6.3, 7.2, 7.3, 8.1, 8.2, 8.3, 10.1, 20.1, 20.3, 21.3
F-6. Science and technology in local, national, and global challenges	46, 49, 51, 52	4		1.4, 4.1, 4.2, 4.3, 4.4, 5.2, 6.2, 6.3, 8.2, 8.3, 16.3, 20.3, 21.3

Benchmark Test 1 Report

Name _____ Date _____ Class _____

National Science Education Standards	Test Items	Number Correct	Proficient? Yes or No	Student Edition Chapter/Lesson
Content Standard G: History and Nature of Science				
G-1. Science as a human endeavor	5	□ / 1		8.3, 9.1, 9.2, 9.3, 9.4, 12.1, 12.2, 12.4, 13.2, 14.1, 14.2, 19.3, 22.1, 24.1, 24.2, 25.1
G-2. Nature of scientific knowledge	5	□ / 1		1.1, 1.5, 2.3, 5.3, 8.3, 9.1, 9.4, 10.2, 11.3, 12.1, 12.2, 12.4, 13.4, 22.1, 24.1, 25.2
G-3. Historical perspectives	5	□ / 1		1.1, 1.2, 1.3, 1.5, 7.1, 9.1, 9.2, 9.3, 10.3, 11.3, 12.1, 12.2, 12.4, 16.2, 22.1, 24.1, 24.2, 24.3, 25.1, 25.2, 25.3

Student Comments: _____

_____

_____

_____

_____

Parent Comments: _____

_____

_____

_____

_____

Teacher Comments: _____

_____

_____

_____

_____

Benchmark Test 1 Report

Name _____ Date _____ Class _____

Benchmark Test 2 Report

National Science Education Standards	Test Items	Number Correct	Proficient? Yes or No	Student Edition Chapter/Lesson
Content Standard A: Science as Inquiry				
A-1. Abilities necessary to do scientific inquiry	39, 42	2		activities, 1.1, 1.2, 1.3, 1.4, 1.5
A-2. Understandings about scientific inquiry	8, 10, 18, 23, 24, 43, 44, 45	8		1.3, 1.5, 2.3, 8.2, 8.3, 8.4, 9.1, 9.4, 11.1, 12.3, 13.1, 14.1, 14.2, 19.1, 19.3, 22.1, 22.3, 23.2, 23.3, 23.4, 24.1, 25.1, 25.2, 25.3
Content Standard B: Physical Science				
B-3. Chemical reactions	14	1		2.1, 3.4, 4.1, 4.3, 5.2, 7.2, 14.2, 21.3, 25.2
B-4. Motion and forces	17, 22	2		16.2, 19.1, 19.2, 22.1, 22.3, 23.1, 25.2
B-5. Conservation of energy and increase in disorder	48	1		17.2, 17.3, 18.1, 18.2, 20.2, 24.3, 25.1
B-6. Interactions of energy and matter	3, 5, 6, 7, 15, 20, 21	8		8.1, 8.2, 8.3, 8.4, 9.4, 16.2, 16.3, 17.2, 24.1, 24.2, 24.3, 25.2
Content Standard C: Life Science				
Content Standard D: Earth Science				
D-1. Energy in the earth system	1, 2, 4, 12, 16, 40, 41, 45, 46, 47, 49, 53, 54, 55	14		1.1, 1.2, 1.4, 3.1, 4.2, 4.3, 5.1, 6.1, 6.3, 9.2, 9.3, 9.4, 10.3, 13.2, 15.1, 16.1, 16.2, 16.3, 17.1, 17.2, 17.3, 18.2, 18.3, 19.1, 19.2, 19.3, 20.1, 21.1, 21.2, 21.3, 23.2, 24.3
D-3. Origin and evolution of the earth system	19, 34, 35	3		1.1, 1.2, 1.4, 2.1, 3.3, 4.1, 7.1, 8.1, 8.2, 8.3, 9.1, 9.2, 9.3, 9.4, 10.1, 11.1, 11.2, 11.3, 12.1, 12.2, 12.3, 12.4, 13.1, 13.2, 13.3, 13.4, 16.3, 17.1, 21.3, 22.1, 22.2, 22.3, 23.1, 24.3

Benchmark Test 2 Report

Name _____ Date _____ Class _____

National Science Education Standards	Test Items	Number Correct	Proficient? Yes or No	Student Edition Chapter/Lesson
Content Standard E: Science and Technology				
E-1. Abilities of technological design	29	☐ / 1		8.4
E-2. Understandings about science and technology	29, 30, 31	☐ / 3		1.3, 4.1, 4.2, 6.2, 8.2, 8.3, 8.4, 9.1, 9.4, 14.1, 14.4, 22.1, 22.3, 23.2, 23.3, 23.4, 24.1, 24.2, 24.3, 25.3
Content Standard F: Science in Personal and Social Perspectives				
F-3. Natural resources	11	☐ / 1		1.4, 4.1, 4.2, 4.3, 4.4, 5.2, 6.3, 14.2, 14.4
F-4. Environmental quality	13	☐ / 1		1.4, 4.1, 4.2, 4.3, 4.4, 5.1, 5.2, 6.3, 17.1
F-5. Natural and human-induced hazards	9, 25, 26, 27, 28, 32, 33, 50, 51, 52	☐ / 10		1.4, 4.1, 4.2, 4.3, 4.4, 5.1, 5.2, 5.3, 6.1, 6.2, 6.3, 7.2, 7.3, 8.1, 8.2, 8.3, 10.1, 20.1, 20.3, 21.3
Content Standard G: History and Nature of Science				
G-1. Science as a human endeavor	36, 37, 38	☐ / 3		8.3, 9.1, 9.2, 9.3, 9.4, 12.1, 12.2, 12.4, 13.2, 14.1, 14.2, 19.3, 22.1, 24.1, 24.2, 25.1
G-2. Nature of scientific knowledge	36, 38, 42, 43	☐ / 4		1.1, 1.5, 2.3, 5.3, 8.3, 9.1, 9.4, 10.2, 11.3, 12.1, 12.2, 12.4, 13.4, 22.1, 24.1, 25.2
G-3. Historical perspectives	37, 39	☐ / 2		1.1, 1.2, 1.3, 1.5, 7.1, 9.1, 9.2, 9.3, 10.3, 11.3, 12.1, 12.2, 12.4, 16.2, 22.1, 24.1, 24.2, 24.3, 25.1, 25.2, 25.3

Benchmark Test 2 Report

Name _____ Date _____ Class _____

Student Comments: _____

_____

_____

_____

_____

_____

_____

Parent Comments: _____

_____

_____

_____

_____

_____

Teacher Comments: _____

_____

_____

_____

_____

_____

_____

Benchmark Test 2 Report

Benchmark Test 3 Report

National Science Education Standards	Test Items	Number Correct	Proficient? Yes or No	Student Edition Chapter/Lesson
Content Standard A: Science as Inquiry				
A-2. Understandings about scientific inquiry	11, 12, 13, 22, 23, 33, 36, 37, 47	▢ 9		1.3, 1.5, 2.3, 8.2, 8.3, 8.4, 9.1, 9.4, 11.1, 12.3, 13.1, 14.1, 14.2, 19.1, 19.3, 22.1, 22.3, 23.2, 23.3, 23.4, 24.1, 25.1, 25.2, 25.3
Content Standard B: Physical Science				
B-2. Structure and properties of matter	39, 40	▢ 2		2.1, 2.2, 2.3, 3.2, 7.1, 12.3, 18.8, 18.3
B-3. Chemical reactions	18, 19, 20, 21, 42, 44, 45	▢ 7		2.1, 3.4, 4.1, 4.3, 5.2, 7.2, 14.2, 21.3, 25.2
B-4. Motion and forces	1, 2, 3, 4, 5, 6	▢ 6		16.2, 19.1, 19.2, 22.1, 22.3, 23.1, 25.2
B-6. Interactions of energy and matter	46	▢ 1		8.1, 8.2, 8.3, 8.4, 9.4, 16.2, 16.3, 17.2, 24.1, 24.2, 24.3, 25.2
Content Standard C: Life Science				
C-1. The cell	25	▢ 1		15.3
C-2. Molecular basis of heredity	25	▢ 1		
C-3. Biological evolution	16, 25, 26, 27, 28, 30, 31	▢ 7		13.2, 13.3, 13.4
C-4. Interdependence of organisms	29, 50	▢ 2		1.2, 1.4, 4.1, 4.2, 4.3, 4.4, 5.2, 6.1, 15.2, 15.3, 16.1, 16.3, 17.1, 21.3
C-5. Matter, energy, and organization in living systems	26, 51, 52, 53, 54, 55	▢ 6		4.1, 15.1, 15.2, 15.3

Benchmark Test 3 Report

National Science Education Standards	Test Items	Number Correct	Proficient? Yes or No	Student Edition Chapter/Lesson
C-6. Behavior of organisms	17, 48, 49	☐ 3		15.2
Content Standard D: Earth Science				
D-1. Energy in the earth system	7, 8, 9, 10, 24, 38	☐ 6		1.1, 1.2, 1.4, 3.1, 4.2, 4.3, 5.1, 6.1, 6.3, 9.2, 9.3, 9.4, 10.3, 13.2, 15.1, 16.1, 16.2, 16.3, 17.1, 17.2, 17.3, 18.2, 18.3, 19.1, 19.2, 19.3, 20.1, 21.1, 21.2, 21.3, 23.2, 24.3
D-2. Geochemical cycles	14, 15	☐ 2		1.4, 2.2. 3.1, 3.3, 3.4, 4.1, 4.3, 5.1, 5.2, 6.1, 7.1, 7.2, 7.3, 8.4, 10.1, 10.2, 10.3, 12.2, 12.3, 14.2, 14.3, 14.4, 15.1, 16.1, 17.2, 18.1
D-3. Origin and evolution of the earth system	32, 34	☐ 2		1.1, 1.2, 1.4, 2.1, 3.3, 4.1, 7.1, 8.1, 8.2, 8.3, 9.1, 9.2, 9.3, 9.4, 10.1, 11.1, 11.2, 11.3, 12.1, 12.2, 12.3, 12.4, 13.1, 13.2, 13.3, 13.4, 16.3, 17.1, 21.3, 22.1, 22.2, 22.3, 23.1, 24.3
Content Standard E: Science and Technology				
E-2. Understandings about science and technology	35	☐ 1		1.3, 4.1, 4.2, 6.2, 8.2, 8.3, 8.4, 9.1, 9.4, 14.1, 14.4, 22.1, 22.3, 23.2, 23.3, 23.4, 24.1, 24.2, 24.3, 25.3
Content Standard F: Science in Personal and Social Perspectives				
F-1. Personal and community health	35	☐ 1		1.4, 4.3
F-3. Natural resources	41, 42, 43	☐ 3		1.4, 4.1, 4.2, 4.3, 4.4, 5.2, 6.3, 14.2, 14.4

Name _____ Date _____ Class _____

National Science Education Standards	Test Items	Number Correct	Proficient? Yes or No	Student Edition Chapter/Lesson
Content Standard G: History and Nature of Science				
G-1. Science as a human endeavor	11, 12, 13, 22, 23	☐ 5		8.3, 9.1, 9.2, 9.3, 9.4, 12.1, 12.2, 12.4, 13.2, 14.1, 14.2, 19.3, 22.1, 24.1, 24.2, 25.1
G-2. Nature of scientific knowledge	12, 13, 22, 23	☐ 4		1.1, 1.5, 2.3, 5.3, 8.3, 9.1, 9.4, 10.2, 11.3, 12.1, 12.2, 12.4, 13.4, 22.1, 24.1, 25.2
G-3. Historical perspectives	22, 23	☐ 2		1.1, 1.2, 1.3, 1.5, 7.1, 9.1, 9.2, 9.3, 10.3, 11.3, 12.1, 12.2, 12.4, 16.2, 22.1, 24.1, 24.2, 24.3, 25.1, 25.2, 25.3

Student Comments: _____

_____

_____

_____

_____

Parent Comments: _____

_____

_____

_____

_____

Teacher Comments: _____

_____

_____

_____

_____

_____

Benchmark Test 3 Report

Name _____ Date _____ Class _____

Benchmark Test 4 Report

National Science Education Standards	Test Items	Number Correct	Proficient? Yes or No	Student Edition Chapter/Lesson
Content Standard A: Science as Inquiry				
A-2. Understandings about scientific inquiry	2, 3, 38, 39, 43, 53, 54, 58, 59	9		1.3, 1.5, 2.3, 8.2, 8.3, 8.4, 9.1, 9.4, 11.1, 12.3, 13.1, 14.1, 14.2, 19.1, 19.3, 22.1, 22.3, 23.2, 23.3, 23.4, 24.1, 25.1, 25.2, 25.3
Content Standard B: Physical Science				
B-4. Motion and forces	9, 10, 12, 42, 45, 48	6		16.2, 19.1, 19.2, 22.1, 22.3, 23.1, 25.2
B-5. Conservation of energy and increase in disorder	22, 23, 24, 25, 26, 30, 37, 40	8		17.2, 17.3, 18.1, 18.2, 20.2, 24.3, 25.1
B-6. Interactions of energy and matter	27, 34, 57	3		8.1, 8.2, 8.3, 8.4, 9.4, 16.2, 16.3, 17.2, 24.1, 24.2, 24.3, 25.2
Content Standard C: Life Science				
Content Standard D: Earth Science				
D-1. Energy in the earth system	1, 4, 5, 6, 7, 8, 11, 13, 14, 16, 17, 18, 19, 20, 21, 28, 31, 32, 33, 35, 36, 41, 44, 46, 47, 49, 50, 51, 52, 55, 56, 60, 61, 62	34		1.1, 1.2, 1.4, 3.1, 4.2, 4.3, 5.1, 6.1, 6.3, 9.2, 9.3, 9.4, 10.3, 13.2, 15.1, 16.1, 16.2, 16.3, 17.1, 17.2, 17.3, 18.2, 18.3, 19.1, 19.2, 19.3, 20.1, 21.1, 21.2, 21.3, 23.2, 24.3
D-3. Origin and evolution of the earth system	29	1		1.1, 1.2, 1.4, 2.1, 3.3, 4.1, 7.1, 8.1, 8.2, 8.3, 9.1, 9.2, 9.3, 9.4, 10.1, 11.1, 11.2, 11.3, 12.1, 12.2, 12.3, 12.4, 13.1, 13.2, 13.3, 13.4, 16.3, 17.1, 21.3, 22.1, 22.2, 22.3, 23.1, 24.3

Name _____ Date _____ Class _____

National Science Education Standards	Test Items	Number Correct	Proficient? Yes or No	Student Edition Chapter/Lesson
Content Standard E: Science and Technology				
E-1. Abilities of technological design	43	☐ 1		8.4
Content Standard F: Science in Personal and Social Perspectives				
F-1. Personal and community health	15	☐ 1		1.4, 4.3
F-4. Environmental quality	15	☐ 1		1.4, 4.1, 4.2, 4.3, 4.4, 5.1, 5.2, 6.3, 17.1
F-6. Science and technology in local, national, and global challenges	15, 18, 19	☐ 3		1.4, 4.1, 4.2, 4.3, 4.4, 5.2, 6.2, 6.3, 8.2, 8.3, 16.3, 20.3, 21.3
Content Standard G: History and Nature of Science				

Student Comments: _____

_____

_____

_____

Parent Comments: _____

_____

_____

_____

Teacher Comments: _____

_____

_____

_____

_____

Benchmark Test 5 Report

National Science Education Standards	Test Items	Number Correct	Proficient? Yes or No	Student Edition Chapter/Lesson
Content Standard A: Science as Inquiry				
A-2. Understandings about scientific inquiry	7, 45	☐ 2		1.3, 1.5, 2.3, 8.2, 8.3, 8.4, 9.1, 9.4, 11.1, 12.3, 13.1, 14.1, 14.2, 19.1, 19.3, 22.1, 22.3, 23.2, 23.3, 23.4, 24.1, 25.1, 25.2, 25.3
Content Standard B: Physical Science				
B-4. Motion and forces	35, 43	☐ 2		16.2, 19.1, 19.2, 22.1, 22.3, 23.1, 25.2
B-6. Interactions of energy and matter	33	☐ 1		8.1, 8.2, 8.3, 8.4, 9.4, 16.2, 16.3, 17.2, 24.1, 24.2, 24.3, 25.2
Content Standard C: Life Science				
C-4. Interdependence of organisms	6	☐ 1		1.2, 1.4, 4.1, 4.2, 4.3, 4.4, 5.2, 6.1, 15.2, 15.3, 16.1, 16.3, 17.1, 21.3
Content Standard D: Earth Science				
D-1. Energy in the earth system	1, 2, 3, 4, 5, 8, 9, 10, 11, 12	☐ 10		1.1, 1.2, 1.4, 3.1, 4.2, 4.3, 5.1, 6.1, 6.3, 9.2, 9.3, 9.4, 10.3, 13.2, 15.1, 16.1, 16.2, 16.3, 17.1, 17.2, 17.3, 18.2, 18.3, 19.1, 19.2, 19.3, 20.1, 21.1, 21.2, 21.3, 23.2, 24.3
D-2. Geochemical cycles	14	☐ 1		1.4, 2.2. 3.1, 3.3, 3.4, 4.1, 4.3, 5.1, 5.2, 6.1, 7.1, 7.2, 7.3, 8.4, 10.1, 10.2, 10.3, 12.2, 12.3, 14.2, 14.3, 14.4, 15.1, 16.1, 17.2, 18.1
D-3. Origin and evolution of the earth system	20, 21, 22, 23, 24, 25, 26, 27, 28, 29, 30, 39, 40, 41	☐ 14		1.1, 1.2, 1.4, 2.1, 3.3, 4.1, 7.1, 8.1, 8.2, 8.3, 9.1, 9.2, 9.3, 9.4, 10.1, 11.1, 11.2, 11.3, 12.1, 12.2, 12.3, 12.4, 13.1, 13.2, 13.3, 13.4, 16.3, 17.1, 21.3, 22.1, 22.2, 22.3, 23.1, 24.3
D-4. Origin and evolution of the universe	31, 32, 34, 44, 46, 47, 48, 49, 50, 51, 52	☐ 11		24.3, 25.1, 25.2, 25.3

Name _____ Date _____ Class _____

National Science Education Standards	Test Items	Number Correct	Proficient? Yes or No	Student Edition Chapter/Lesson
Content Standard E: Science and Technology				
E-1. Abilities of technological design	36, 37, 38	☐ 3		8.4
E-2. Understandings about science and technology	36, 37, 38, 42	☐ 4		1.3, 4.1, 4.2, 6.2, 8.2, 8.3, 8.4, 9.1, 9.4, 14.1, 14.4, 22.1, 22.3, 23.2, 23.3, 23.4, 24.1, 24.2, 24.3, 25.3
Content Standard F: Science in Personal and Social Perspectives				
F-5. Natural and human-induced hazards	13, 15, 16	☐ 3		1.4, 4.1, 4.2, 4.3, 4.4, 5.1, 5.2, 5.3, 6.1, 6.2, 6.3, 7.2, 7.3, 8.1, 8.2, 8.3, 10.1, 20.1, 20.3, 21.3
F-6. Science and technology in local, national, and global challenges	15, 16	☐ 2		1.4, 4.1, 4.2, 4.3, 4.4, 5.2, 6.2, 6.3, 8.2, 8.3, 16.3, 20.3, 21.3
Content Standard G: History and Nature of Science				
G-3. Historical perspectives	17, 18, 19	☐ 3		1.1, 1.2, 1.3, 1.5, 7.1, 9.1, 9.2, 9.3, 10.3, 11.3, 12.1, 12.2, 12.4, 16.2, 22.1, 24.1, 24.2, 24.3, 25.1, 25.2, 25.3

Student Comments: _____

_____

_____

Parent Comments: _____

_____

_____

Teacher Comments: _____

_____

_____

Benchmark Test 5 Report

Name _____ Date _____ Class _____

National Science Education Standards	Test Items	Number Correct	Proficient? Yes or No	Student Edition Chapter/Lesson
Content Standard A: Science as Inquiry				
A-1. Abilities necessary to do scientific inquiry	3	☐ 1		activities, 1.1, 1.2, 1.3, 1.4, 1.5
A-2. Understandings about scientific inquiry	1, 2, 3, 9, 18, 24, 32, 33, 43, 37, 38, 40, 46	☐ 13		1.3, 1.5, 2.3, 8.2, 8.3, 8.4, 9.1, 9.4, 11.1, 12.3, 13.1, 14.1, 14.2, 19.1, 19.3, 22.1, 22.3, 23.2, 23.3, 23.4, 24.1, 25.1, 25.2, 25.3
Content Standard B: Physical Science				
B-2. Structure and properties of matter	5, 6, 8	☐ 3		2.1, 2.2, 2.3, 3.2, 7.1, 12.3, 18.8, 18.3
B-3. Chemical reactions	4	☐ 1		2.1, 3.4, 4.1, 4.3, 5.2, 7.2, 14.2, 21.3, 25.2
B-4. Motion and forces	14, 29, 30, 42, 47	☐ 5		16.2, 19.1, 19.2, 22.1, 22.3, 23.1, 25.2
B-5. Conservation of energy and increase in disorder	43	☐ 1		17.2, 17.3, 18.1, 18.2, 20.2, 24.3, 25.1
B-6. Interactions of energy and matter	16, 19	☐ 2		8.1, 8.2, 8.3, 8.4, 9.4, 16.2, 16.3, 17.2, 24.1, 24.2, 24.3, 25.2
Content Standard C: Life Science				
C-3. Biological evolution	35, 36	☐ 2		13.2, 13.3, 13.4
C-6. Behavior of organisms	39	☐ 1		15.2
Content Standard D: Earth Science				
D-1. Energy in the earth system	15, 23, 25, 26, 28, 31, 41, 42, 45, 48, 49, 50, 51, 52	☐ 14		1.1, 1.2, 1.4, 3.1, 4.2, 4.3, 5.1, 6.1, 6.3, 9.2, 9.3, 9.4, 10.3, 13.2, 15.1, 16.1, 16.2, 16.3, 17.1, 17.2, 17.3, 18.2, 18.3, 19.1, 19.2, 19.3, 20.1, 21.1, 21.2, 21.3, 23.2, 24.3

Outcome Test Report

National Science Education Standards	Test Items	Number Correct	Proficient? Yes or No	Student Edition Chapter/Lesson
D-2. Geochemical cycles	7, 12	□ 2		1.4, 2.2. 3.1, 3.3, 3.4, 4.1, 4.3, 5.1, 5.2, 6.1, 7.1, 7.2, 7.3, 8.4, 10.1, 10.2, 10.3, 12.2, 12.3, 14.2, 14.3, 14.4, 15.1, 16.1, 17.2, 18.1
D-3. Origin and evolution of the earth system	53, 54, 55, 56, 57, 58, 59	□ 7		1.1, 1.2, 1.4, 2.1, 3.3, 4.1, 7.1, 8.1, 8.2, 8.3, 9.1, 9.2, 9.3, 9.4, 10.1, 11.1, 11.2, 11.3, 12.1, 12.2, 12.3, 12.4, 13.1, 13.2, 13.3, 13.4, 16.3, 17.1, 21.3, 22.1, 22.2, 22.3, 23.1, 24.3
D-4. Origin and evolution of the universe	60	□ 1		24.3, 25.1, 25.2, 25.3
Content Standard E: Science and Technology				
E-2. Understandings about science and technology	11, 21	□ 2		1.3, 4.1, 4.2, 6.2, 8.2, 8.3, 8.4, 9.1, 9.4, 14.1, 14.4, 22.1, 22.3, 23.2, 23.3, 23.4, 24.1, 24.2, 24.3, 25.3
Content Standard F: Science in Personal and Social Perspectives				
F-1. Personal and community health	11	□ 1		1.4, 4.3
F-3. Natural resources	10, 13, 17	□ 3		1.4, 4.1, 4.2, 4.3, 4.4, 5.2, 6.3, 14.2, 14.4
F-5. Natural and human-induced hazards	20, 22, 27, 52	□ 4		1.4, 4.1, 4.2, 4.3, 4.4, 5.1, 5.2, 5.3, 6.1, 6.2, 6.3, 7.2, 7.3, 8.1, 8.2, 8.3, 10.1, 20.1, 20.3, 21.3
F-6. Science and technology in local, national, and global challenges	11, 12	□ 2		1.4, 4.1, 4.2, 4.3, 4.4, 5.2, 6.2, 6.3, 8.2, 8.3, 16.3, 20.3, 21.3
Content Standard G: History and Nature of Science				
G-1. Science as a human endeavor	24, 32, 33, 34	□ 4		8.3, 9.1, 9.2, 9.3, 9.4, 12.1, 12.2, 12.4, 13.2, 14.1, 14.2, 19.3, 22.1, 24.1, 24.2, 25.1
G-2. Nature of scientific knowledge	24, 32, 33, 34	□ 4		1.1, 1.5, 2.3, 5.3, 8.3, 9.1, 9.4, 10.2, 11.3, 12.1, 12.2, 12.4, 13.4, 22.1, 24.1, 25.2

Outcome Test Report

Name _____ Date _____ Class _____

National Science Education Standards	Test Items	Number Correct	Proficient? Yes or No	Student Edition Chapter/ Lesson
G-3. Historical perspectives	24, 34	☐ / 2		1.1, 1.2, 1.3, 1.5, 7.1, 9.1, 9.2, 9.3, 10.3, 11.3, 12.1, 12.2, 12.4, 16.2, 22.1, 24.1, 24.2, 24.3, 25.1, 25.2, 25.3

Student Comments: _____

_____

_____

_____

_____

_____

Parent Comments: _____

_____

_____

_____

_____

_____

Teacher Comments: _____

_____

_____

_____

_____

_____

Outcome Test Report

Practice Test 1 Report

National Science Education Standards	Test Items	Number Correct	Proficient? Yes or No	Student Edition Chapter/Lesson
Content Standard A: Science as Inquiry				
A-1. Abilities necessary to do scientific inquiry	23	☐ 1		activities, 1.1, 1.2, 1.3, 1.4, 1.5
A-2. Understandings about scientific inquiry	23	☐ 1		1.3, 1.5, 2.3, 8.2, 8.3, 8.4, 9.1, 9.4, 11.1, 12.3, 13.1, 14.1, 14.2, 19.1, 19.3, 22.1, 22.3, 23.2, 23.3, 23.4, 24.1, 25.1, 25.2, 25.3
Content Standard B: Physical Science				
B-2. Structure and properties of matter	2	☐ 1		2.1, 2.2, 2.3, 3.2, 7.1, 12.3, 18.8, 18.3
B-3. Chemical reactions	24	☐ 1		2.1, 3.4, 4.1, 4.3, 5.2, 7.2, 14.2, 21.3, 25.2
B-4. Motion and forces	17	☐ 1		16.2, 19.1, 19.2, 22.1, 22.3, 23.1, 25.2
B-5. Conservation of energy and increase in disorder	21, 26, 35, 47	☐ 4		17.2, 17.3, 18.1, 18.2, 20.2, 24.3, 25.1
Content Standard C: Life Science				
C-3. Biological evolution	13	☐ 1		13.2, 13.3, 13.4
C-5. Matter, energy, and organization in living systems	41	☐ 1		4.1, 15.1, 15.2, 15.3
C-6. Behavior of organisms	29, 38	☐ 2		15.2
Content Standard D: Earth Science				
D-1. Energy in the earth system	3, 8, 9, 10, 30, 31, 33, 37, 48	☐ 9		1.1, 1.2, 1.4, 3.1, 4.2, 4.3, 5.1, 6.1, 6.3, 9.2, 9.3, 9.4, 10.3, 13.2, 15.1, 16.1, 16.2, 16.3, 17.1, 17.2, 17.3, 18.2, 18.3, 19.1, 19.2, 19.3, 20.1, 21.1, 21.2, 21.3, 23.2, 24.3

Practice Test 1 Report

Name _____ Date _____ Class _____

National Science Education Standards	Test Items	Number Correct	Proficient? Yes or No	Student Edition Chapter/Lesson
D-2. Geochemical cycles	1, 5, 6	☐ 3		1.4, 2.2. 3.1, 3.3, 3.4, 4.1, 4.3, 5.1, 5.2, 6.1, 7.1, 7.2, 7.3, 8.4, 10.1, 10.2, 10.3, 12.2, 12.3, 14.2, 14.3, 14.4, 15.1, 16.1, 17.2, 18.1
D-3. Origin and evolution of the earth system	11, 12, 14, 32, 42, 43, 44	☐ 7		1.1, 1.2, 1.4, 2.1, 3.3, 4.1, 7.1, 8.1, 8.2, 8.3, 9.1, 9.2, 9.3, 9.4, 10.1, 11.1, 11.2, 11.3, 12.1, 12.2, 12.3, 12.4, 13.1, 13.2, 13.3, 13.4, 16.3, 17.1, 21.3, 22.1, 22.2, 22.3, 23.1, 24.3
D-4. Origin and evolution of the universe	39, 40, 45, 46, 49, 50, 51	☐ 7		24.3, 25.1, 25.2, 25.3
Content Standard E: Science and Technology				
E-1. Abilities of technological design	28	☐ 1		8.4
E-2. Understandings about science and technology	28	☐ 1		1.3, 4.1, 4.2, 6.2, 8.2, 8.3, 8.4, 9.1, 9.4, 14.1, 14.4, 22.1, 22.3, 23.2, 23.3, 23.4, 24.1, 24.2, 24.3, 25.3
Content Standard F: Science in Personal and Social Perspectives				
F-2. Population growth	4	☐ 1		1.4, 4.1, 4.2, 4.4
F-3. Natural resources	7, 15	☐ 2		1.4, 4.1, 4.2, 4.3, 4.4, 5.2, 6.3, 14.2, 14.4
F-4. Environmental quality	20, 22, 34	☐ 3		1.4, 4.1, 4.2, 4.3, 4.4, 5.1, 5.2, 6.3, 17.1
F-5. Natural and human-induced hazards	18, 25, 27, 36, 25	☐ 5		1.4, 4.1, 4.2, 4.3, 4.4, 5.1, 5.2, 5.3, 6.1, 6.2, 6.3, 7.2, 7.3, 8.1, 8.2, 8.3, 10.1, 20.1, 20.3, 21.3
F-6. Science and technology in local, national, and global challenges	16, 19	☐ 2		1.4, 4.1, 4.2, 4.3, 4.4, 5.2, 6.2, 6.3, 8.2, 8.3, 16.3, 20.3, 21.3
Content Standard G: History and Nature of Science				
G-1. Science as a human endeavor	23	☐ 1		8.3, 9.1, 9.2, 9.3, 9.4, 12.1, 12.2, 12.4, 13.2, 14.1, 14.2, 19.3, 22.1, 24.1, 24.2, 25.1

Practice Test 1 Report

Name _____ Date _____ Class _____

National Science Education Standards	Test Items	Number Correct	Proficient? Yes or No	Student Edition Chapter/Lesson
G-2. Nature of scientific knowledge	23	☐ 1		1.1, 1.5, 2.3, 5.3, 8.3, 9.1, 9.4, 10.2, 11.3, 12.1, 12.2, 12.4, 13.4, 22.1, 24.1, 25.2
G-3. Historical perspectives	23	☐ 1		1.1, 1.2, 1.3, 1.5, 7.1, 9.1, 9.2, 9.3, 10.3, 11.3, 12.1, 12.2, 12.4, 16.2, 22.1, 24.1, 24.2, 24.3, 25.1, 25.2, 25.3

Student Comments: _____

_____

_____

_____

_____

_____

Parent Comments: _____

_____

_____

_____

_____

_____

Teacher Comments: _____

_____

_____

_____

_____

_____

Practice Test 1 Report

Name _____ Date _____ Class _____

Practice Test 2 Report

National Science Education Standards	Test Items	Number Correct	Proficient? Yes or No	Student Edition Chapter/Lesson
Content Standard A: Science as Inquiry				
A-1. Abilities necessary to do scientific inquiry	23, 44, 46	☐ 3		activities, 1.1, 1.2, 1.3, 1.4, 1.5
A-2. Understandings about scientific inquiry	5, 23, 44, 46	☐ 4		1.3, 1.5, 2.3, 8.2, 8.3, 8.4, 9.1, 9.4, 11.1, 12.3, 13.1, 14.1, 14.2, 19.1, 19.3, 22.1, 22.3, 23.2, 23.3, 23.4, 24.1, 25.1, 25.2, 25.3
Content Standard B: Physical Science				
B-1. Structure of atoms	24	☐ 1		2.1, 4.2, 5.1, 24.3, 25.2
B-2. Structure and properties of matter	9	☐ 1		2.1, 2.2, 2.3, 3.2, 7.1, 12.3, 18.8, 18.3
B-3. Chemical reactions	1, 42, 49	☐ 3		2.1, 3.4, 4.1, 4.3, 5.2, 7.2, 14.2, 21.3, 25.2
Content Standard C: Life Science				
C-1. The cell	14	☐ 1		15.3
C-3. Biological evolution	6, 16	☐ 2		13.2, 13.3, 13.4
C-4. Interdependence of organisms	2	☐ 1		1.2, 1.4, 4.1, 4.2, 4.3, 4.4, 5.2, 6.1, 15.2, 15.3, 16.1, 16.3, 17.1, 21.3
C-5. Matter, energy, and organization in living systems	10, 28	☐ 2		4.1, 15.1, 15.2, 15.3
Content Standard D: Earth Science				
D-1. Energy in the earth system	3, 4, 12, 13, 15, 17, 18, 27, 30, 32, 33, 34, 38	☐ 13		1.1, 1.2, 1.4, 3.1, 4.2, 4.3, 5.1, 6.1, 6.3, 9.2, 9.3, 9.4, 10.3, 13.2, 15.1, 16.1, 16.2, 16.3, 17.1, 17.2, 17.3, 18.2, 18.3, 19.1, 19.2, 19.3, 20.1, 21.1, 21.2, 21.3, 23.2, 24.3

Practice Test 2 Report

National Science Education Standards	Test Items	Number Correct	Proficient? Yes or No	Student Edition Chapter/Lesson
D-2. Geochemical cycles	26	☐ 1		1.4, 2.2. 3.1, 3.3, 3.4, 4.1, 4.3, 5.1, 5.2, 6.1, 7.1, 7.2, 7.3, 8.4, 10.1, 10.2, 10.3, 12.2, 12.3, 14.2, 14.3, 14.4, 15.1, 16.1, 17.2, 18.1
D-3. Origin and evolution of the earth system	7, 26, 36, 39, 40, 41, 45	☐ 7		1.1, 1.2, 1.4, 2.1, 3.3, 4.1, 7.1, 8.1, 8.2, 8.3, 9.1, 9.2, 9.3, 9.4, 10.1, 11.1, 11.2, 11.3, 12.1, 12.2, 12.3, 12.4, 13.1, 13.2, 13.3, 13.4, 16.3, 17.1, 21.3, 22.1, 22.2, 22.3, 23.1, 24.3
D-4. Origin and evolution of the universe	19, 43, 47, 48, 50, 51	☐ 6		24.3, 25.1, 25.2, 25.3
Content Standard E: Science and Technology				
Content Standard F: Science in Personal and Social Perspectives				
F-1. Personal and community health	20, 35	☐ 2		1.4, 4.3
F-3. Natural resources	11, 20, 22, 29	☐ 4		1.4, 4.1, 4.2, 4.3, 4.4, 5.2, 6.3, 14.2, 14.4
F-5. Natural and human-induced hazards	8, 21, 37	☐ 3		1.4, 4.1, 4.2, 4.3, 4.4, 5.1, 5.2, 5.3, 6.1, 6.2, 6.3, 7.2, 7.3, 8.1, 8.2, 8.3, 10.1, 20.1, 20.3, 21.3
Content Standard G: History and Nature of Science				
G-1. Science as a human endeavor	23, 46	☐ 2		8.3, 9.1, 9.2, 9.3, 9.4, 12.1, 12.2, 12.4, 13.2, 14.1, 14.2, 19.3, 22.1, 24.1, 24.2, 25.1
G-2. Nature of scientific knowledge	23	☐ 1		1.1, 1.5, 2.3, 5.3, 8.3, 9.1, 9.4, 10.2, 11.3, 12.1, 12.2, 12.4, 13.4, 22.1, 24.1, 25.2
G-3. Historical perspectives	31, 44	☐ 2		1.1, 1.2, 1.3, 1.5, 7.1, 9.1, 9.2, 9.3, 10.3, 11.3, 12.1, 12.2, 12.4, 16.2, 22.1, 24.1, 24.2, 24.3, 25.1, 25.2, 25.3

Name _____ Date _____ Class _____

Student Comments: _____

_____

_____

_____

_____

_____

_____

Parent Comments: _____

_____

_____

_____

_____

_____

_____

Teacher Comments: _____

_____

_____

_____

_____

_____

_____

Practice Test 2 Report

Name _____ Date _____ Class _____

Answer Sheet

1. Ⓐ	Ⓑ	Ⓒ	Ⓓ	34. Ⓐ	Ⓑ	Ⓒ	Ⓓ
2. Ⓐ	Ⓑ	Ⓒ	Ⓓ	35. Ⓐ	Ⓑ	Ⓒ	Ⓓ
3. Ⓐ	Ⓑ	Ⓒ	Ⓓ	36. Ⓐ	Ⓑ	Ⓒ	Ⓓ
4. Ⓐ	Ⓑ	Ⓒ	Ⓓ	37. Ⓐ	Ⓑ	Ⓒ	Ⓓ
5. Ⓐ	Ⓑ	Ⓒ	Ⓓ	38. Ⓐ	Ⓑ	Ⓒ	Ⓓ
6. Ⓐ	Ⓑ	Ⓒ	Ⓓ	39. Ⓐ	Ⓑ	Ⓒ	Ⓓ
7. Ⓐ	Ⓑ	Ⓒ	Ⓓ	40. Ⓐ	Ⓑ	Ⓒ	Ⓓ
8. Ⓐ	Ⓑ	Ⓒ	Ⓓ	41. Ⓐ	Ⓑ	Ⓒ	Ⓓ
9. Ⓐ	Ⓑ	Ⓒ	Ⓓ	42. Ⓐ	Ⓑ	Ⓒ	Ⓓ
10. Ⓐ	Ⓑ	Ⓒ	Ⓓ	43. Ⓐ	Ⓑ	Ⓒ	Ⓓ
11. Ⓐ	Ⓑ	Ⓒ	Ⓓ	44. Ⓐ	Ⓑ	Ⓒ	Ⓓ
12. Ⓐ	Ⓑ	Ⓒ	Ⓓ	45. Ⓐ	Ⓑ	Ⓒ	Ⓓ
13. Ⓐ	Ⓑ	Ⓒ	Ⓓ	46. Ⓐ	Ⓑ	Ⓒ	Ⓓ
14. Ⓐ	Ⓑ	Ⓒ	Ⓓ	47. Ⓐ	Ⓑ	Ⓒ	Ⓓ
15. Ⓐ	Ⓑ	Ⓒ	Ⓓ	48. Ⓐ	Ⓑ	Ⓒ	Ⓓ
16. Ⓐ	Ⓑ	Ⓒ	Ⓓ	49. Ⓐ	Ⓑ	Ⓒ	Ⓓ
17. Ⓐ	Ⓑ	Ⓒ	Ⓓ	50. Ⓐ	Ⓑ	Ⓒ	Ⓓ
18. Ⓐ	Ⓑ	Ⓒ	Ⓓ	51. Ⓐ	Ⓑ	Ⓒ	Ⓓ
19. Ⓐ	Ⓑ	Ⓒ	Ⓓ	52. Ⓐ	Ⓑ	Ⓒ	Ⓓ
20. Ⓐ	Ⓑ	Ⓒ	Ⓓ	53. Ⓐ	Ⓑ	Ⓒ	Ⓓ
21. Ⓐ	Ⓑ	Ⓒ	Ⓓ	54. Ⓐ	Ⓑ	Ⓒ	Ⓓ
22. Ⓐ	Ⓑ	Ⓒ	Ⓓ	55. Ⓐ	Ⓑ	Ⓒ	Ⓓ
23. Ⓐ	Ⓑ	Ⓒ	Ⓓ	56. Ⓐ	Ⓑ	Ⓒ	Ⓓ
24. Ⓐ	Ⓑ	Ⓒ	Ⓓ	57. Ⓐ	Ⓑ	Ⓒ	Ⓓ
25. Ⓐ	Ⓑ	Ⓒ	Ⓓ	58. Ⓐ	Ⓑ	Ⓒ	Ⓓ
26. Ⓐ	Ⓑ	Ⓒ	Ⓓ	59. Ⓐ	Ⓑ	Ⓒ	Ⓓ
27. Ⓐ	Ⓑ	Ⓒ	Ⓓ	60. Ⓐ	Ⓑ	Ⓒ	Ⓓ
28. Ⓐ	Ⓑ	Ⓒ	Ⓓ	61. Ⓐ	Ⓑ	Ⓒ	Ⓓ
29. Ⓐ	Ⓑ	Ⓒ	Ⓓ	62. Ⓐ	Ⓑ	Ⓒ	Ⓓ
30. Ⓐ	Ⓑ	Ⓒ	Ⓓ	63. Ⓐ	Ⓑ	Ⓒ	Ⓓ
31. Ⓐ	Ⓑ	Ⓒ	Ⓓ	64. Ⓐ	Ⓑ	Ⓒ	Ⓓ
32. Ⓐ	Ⓑ	Ⓒ	Ⓓ	65. Ⓐ	Ⓑ	Ⓒ	Ⓓ
33. Ⓐ	Ⓑ	Ⓒ	Ⓓ				

Answer Sheet

Name _____ Date _____ Class _____

Answer Sheet

1. Ⓐ Ⓑ Ⓒ Ⓓ
2. Ⓕ Ⓖ Ⓗ Ⓙ
3. Ⓐ Ⓑ Ⓒ Ⓓ
4. Ⓕ Ⓖ Ⓗ Ⓙ
5. Ⓐ Ⓑ Ⓒ Ⓓ
6. Ⓕ Ⓖ Ⓗ Ⓙ
7. Ⓐ Ⓑ Ⓒ Ⓓ
8. Ⓕ Ⓖ Ⓗ Ⓙ
9. Ⓐ Ⓑ Ⓒ Ⓓ
10. Ⓕ Ⓖ Ⓗ Ⓙ
11. Ⓐ Ⓑ Ⓒ Ⓓ
12. Ⓕ Ⓖ Ⓗ Ⓙ
13. Ⓐ Ⓑ Ⓒ Ⓓ
14. Ⓕ Ⓖ Ⓗ Ⓙ
15. Ⓐ Ⓑ Ⓒ Ⓓ
16. Ⓕ Ⓖ Ⓗ Ⓙ
17. Ⓐ Ⓑ Ⓒ Ⓓ
18. Ⓕ Ⓖ Ⓗ Ⓙ
19. Ⓐ Ⓑ Ⓒ Ⓓ
20. Ⓕ Ⓖ Ⓗ Ⓙ
21. Ⓐ Ⓑ Ⓒ Ⓓ
22. Ⓕ Ⓖ Ⓗ Ⓙ
23. Ⓐ Ⓑ Ⓒ Ⓓ
24. Ⓕ Ⓖ Ⓗ Ⓙ
25. Ⓐ Ⓑ Ⓒ Ⓓ
26. Ⓕ Ⓖ Ⓗ Ⓙ
27. Ⓐ Ⓑ Ⓒ Ⓓ
28. Ⓕ Ⓖ Ⓗ Ⓙ
29. Ⓐ Ⓑ Ⓒ Ⓓ
30. Ⓕ Ⓖ Ⓗ Ⓙ

31. Ⓐ Ⓑ Ⓒ Ⓓ
32. Ⓕ Ⓖ Ⓗ Ⓙ
33. Ⓐ Ⓑ Ⓒ Ⓓ
34. Ⓕ Ⓖ Ⓗ Ⓙ
35. Ⓐ Ⓑ Ⓒ Ⓓ
36. Ⓕ Ⓖ Ⓗ Ⓙ
37. Ⓐ Ⓑ Ⓒ Ⓓ
38. Ⓕ Ⓖ Ⓗ Ⓙ
39. Ⓐ Ⓑ Ⓒ Ⓓ
40. Ⓕ Ⓖ Ⓗ Ⓙ
41. Ⓐ Ⓑ Ⓒ Ⓓ
42. Ⓕ Ⓖ Ⓗ Ⓙ
43. Ⓐ Ⓑ Ⓒ Ⓓ
44. Ⓕ Ⓖ Ⓗ Ⓙ
45. Ⓐ Ⓑ Ⓒ Ⓓ
46. Ⓕ Ⓖ Ⓗ Ⓙ
47. Ⓐ Ⓑ Ⓒ Ⓓ
48. Ⓕ Ⓖ Ⓗ Ⓙ
49. Ⓐ Ⓑ Ⓒ Ⓓ
50. Ⓕ Ⓖ Ⓗ Ⓙ
51. Ⓐ Ⓑ Ⓒ Ⓓ
52. Ⓕ Ⓖ Ⓗ Ⓙ
53. Ⓐ Ⓑ Ⓒ Ⓓ
54. Ⓕ Ⓖ Ⓗ Ⓙ
55. Ⓐ Ⓑ Ⓒ Ⓓ
56. Ⓕ Ⓖ Ⓗ Ⓙ
57. Ⓐ Ⓑ Ⓒ Ⓓ
58. Ⓕ Ⓖ Ⓗ Ⓙ
59. Ⓐ Ⓑ Ⓒ Ⓓ
60. Ⓕ Ⓖ Ⓗ Ⓙ

Answer Sheet

1.	Ⓐ	Ⓑ	Ⓒ	Ⓓ	Ⓔ		41.	Ⓐ	Ⓑ	Ⓒ	Ⓓ	Ⓔ
2.	Ⓐ	Ⓑ	Ⓒ	Ⓓ	Ⓔ		42.	Ⓐ	Ⓑ	Ⓒ	Ⓓ	Ⓔ
3.	Ⓐ	Ⓑ	Ⓒ	Ⓓ	Ⓔ		43.	Ⓐ	Ⓑ	Ⓒ	Ⓓ	Ⓔ
4.	Ⓐ	Ⓑ	Ⓒ	Ⓓ	Ⓔ		44.	Ⓐ	Ⓑ	Ⓒ	Ⓓ	Ⓔ
5.	Ⓐ	Ⓑ	Ⓒ	Ⓓ	Ⓔ		45.	Ⓐ	Ⓑ	Ⓒ	Ⓓ	Ⓔ
6.	Ⓐ	Ⓑ	Ⓒ	Ⓓ	Ⓔ		46.	Ⓐ	Ⓑ	Ⓒ	Ⓓ	Ⓔ
7.	Ⓐ	Ⓑ	Ⓒ	Ⓓ	Ⓔ		47.	Ⓐ	Ⓑ	Ⓒ	Ⓓ	Ⓔ
8.	Ⓐ	Ⓑ	Ⓒ	Ⓓ	Ⓔ		48.	Ⓐ	Ⓑ	Ⓒ	Ⓓ	Ⓔ
9.	Ⓐ	Ⓑ	Ⓒ	Ⓓ	Ⓔ		49.	Ⓐ	Ⓑ	Ⓒ	Ⓓ	Ⓔ
10.	Ⓐ	Ⓑ	Ⓒ	Ⓓ	Ⓔ		50.	Ⓐ	Ⓑ	Ⓒ	Ⓓ	Ⓔ
11.	Ⓐ	Ⓑ	Ⓒ	Ⓓ	Ⓔ		51.	Ⓐ	Ⓑ	Ⓒ	Ⓓ	Ⓔ
12.	Ⓐ	Ⓑ	Ⓒ	Ⓓ	Ⓔ		52.	Ⓐ	Ⓑ	Ⓒ	Ⓓ	Ⓔ
13.	Ⓐ	Ⓑ	Ⓒ	Ⓓ	Ⓔ		53.	Ⓐ	Ⓑ	Ⓒ	Ⓓ	Ⓔ
14.	Ⓐ	Ⓑ	Ⓒ	Ⓓ	Ⓔ		54.	Ⓐ	Ⓑ	Ⓒ	Ⓓ	Ⓔ
15.	Ⓐ	Ⓑ	Ⓒ	Ⓓ	Ⓔ		55.	Ⓐ	Ⓑ	Ⓒ	Ⓓ	Ⓔ
16.	Ⓐ	Ⓑ	Ⓒ	Ⓓ	Ⓔ		56.	Ⓐ	Ⓑ	Ⓒ	Ⓓ	Ⓔ
17.	Ⓐ	Ⓑ	Ⓒ	Ⓓ	Ⓔ		57.	Ⓐ	Ⓑ	Ⓒ	Ⓓ	Ⓔ
18.	Ⓐ	Ⓑ	Ⓒ	Ⓓ	Ⓔ		58.	Ⓐ	Ⓑ	Ⓒ	Ⓓ	Ⓔ
19.	Ⓐ	Ⓑ	Ⓒ	Ⓓ	Ⓔ		59.	Ⓐ	Ⓑ	Ⓒ	Ⓓ	Ⓔ
20.	Ⓐ	Ⓑ	Ⓒ	Ⓓ	Ⓔ		60.	Ⓐ	Ⓑ	Ⓒ	Ⓓ	Ⓔ
21.	Ⓐ	Ⓑ	Ⓒ	Ⓓ	Ⓔ		61.	Ⓐ	Ⓑ	Ⓒ	Ⓓ	Ⓔ
22.	Ⓐ	Ⓑ	Ⓒ	Ⓓ	Ⓔ		62.	Ⓐ	Ⓑ	Ⓒ	Ⓓ	Ⓔ
23.	Ⓐ	Ⓑ	Ⓒ	Ⓓ	Ⓔ		63.	Ⓐ	Ⓑ	Ⓒ	Ⓓ	Ⓔ
24.	Ⓐ	Ⓑ	Ⓒ	Ⓓ	Ⓔ		64.	Ⓐ	Ⓑ	Ⓒ	Ⓓ	Ⓔ
25.	Ⓐ	Ⓑ	Ⓒ	Ⓓ	Ⓔ		65.	Ⓐ	Ⓑ	Ⓒ	Ⓓ	Ⓔ
26.	Ⓐ	Ⓑ	Ⓒ	Ⓓ	Ⓔ		66.	Ⓐ	Ⓑ	Ⓒ	Ⓓ	Ⓔ
27.	Ⓐ	Ⓑ	Ⓒ	Ⓓ	Ⓔ		67.	Ⓐ	Ⓑ	Ⓒ	Ⓓ	Ⓔ
28.	Ⓐ	Ⓑ	Ⓒ	Ⓓ	Ⓔ		68.	Ⓐ	Ⓑ	Ⓒ	Ⓓ	Ⓔ
29.	Ⓐ	Ⓑ	Ⓒ	Ⓓ	Ⓔ		69.	Ⓐ	Ⓑ	Ⓒ	Ⓓ	Ⓔ
30.	Ⓐ	Ⓑ	Ⓒ	Ⓓ	Ⓔ		70.	Ⓐ	Ⓑ	Ⓒ	Ⓓ	Ⓔ
31.	Ⓐ	Ⓑ	Ⓒ	Ⓓ	Ⓔ		71.	Ⓐ	Ⓑ	Ⓒ	Ⓓ	Ⓔ
32.	Ⓐ	Ⓑ	Ⓒ	Ⓓ	Ⓔ		72.	Ⓐ	Ⓑ	Ⓒ	Ⓓ	Ⓔ
33.	Ⓐ	Ⓑ	Ⓒ	Ⓓ	Ⓔ		73.	Ⓐ	Ⓑ	Ⓒ	Ⓓ	Ⓔ
34.	Ⓐ	Ⓑ	Ⓒ	Ⓓ	Ⓔ		74.	Ⓐ	Ⓑ	Ⓒ	Ⓓ	Ⓔ
35.	Ⓐ	Ⓑ	Ⓒ	Ⓓ	Ⓔ		75.	Ⓐ	Ⓑ	Ⓒ	Ⓓ	Ⓔ
36.	Ⓐ	Ⓑ	Ⓒ	Ⓓ	Ⓔ		76.	Ⓐ	Ⓑ	Ⓒ	Ⓓ	Ⓔ
37.	Ⓐ	Ⓑ	Ⓒ	Ⓓ	Ⓔ		77.	Ⓐ	Ⓑ	Ⓒ	Ⓓ	Ⓔ
38.	Ⓐ	Ⓑ	Ⓒ	Ⓓ	Ⓔ		78.	Ⓐ	Ⓑ	Ⓒ	Ⓓ	Ⓔ
39.	Ⓐ	Ⓑ	Ⓒ	Ⓓ	Ⓔ		79.	Ⓐ	Ⓑ	Ⓒ	Ⓓ	Ⓔ
40.	Ⓐ	Ⓑ	Ⓒ	Ⓓ	Ⓔ		80.	Ⓐ	Ⓑ	Ⓒ	Ⓓ	Ⓔ

Answer Sheet

Answers

Diagnostic Test A

1. C	37. C	73. A	109. D
2. A	38. D	74. A	110. B
3. B	39. B	75. D	111. B
4. D	40. B	76. B	112. B
5. A	41. C	77. D	113. A
6. C	42. A	78. A	114. A
7. A	43. D	79. B	115. D
8. A	44. B	80. D	116. D
9. D	45. B	81. C	117. A
10. B	46. A	82. C	118. D
11. A	47. D	83. A	119. A
12. D	48. D	84. B	120. B
13. D	49. A	85. C	121. A
14. C	50. C	86. B	122. C
15. B	51. D	87. C	123. D
16. A	52. B	88. D	124. B
17. B	53. A	89. B	125. A
18. C	54. C	90. D	126. B
19. D	55. A	91. B	127. D
20. C	56. B	92. A	128. B
21. C	57. B	93. C	129. A
22. C	58. C	94. C	130. C
23. C	59. C	95. D	131. C
24. D	60. D	96. A	132. C
25. A	61. D	97. B	133. D
26. C	62. C	98. D	134. A
27. D	63. B	99. D	135. C
28. B	64. B	100. C	136. D
29. C	65. D	101. D	137. D
30. A	66. A	102. D	138. B
31. B	67. C	103. D	139. D
32. B	68. C	104. A	140. C
33. C	69. B	105. D	141. B
34. D	70. B	106. B	142. C
35. D	71. D	107. B	143. D
36. C	72. C	108. C	

Diagnostic Test B

1. B	37. B	73. A	109. D
2. A	38. B	74. A	110. B
3. B	39. D	75. D	111. B
4. C	40. C	76. B	112. A
5. D	41. C	77. A	113. D
6. B	42. B	78. A	114. C
7. D	43. D	79. A	115. C
8. B	44. B	80. D	116. D
9. A	45. B	81. D	117. C
10. D	46. C	82. C	118. D
11. C	47. A	83. D	119. A
12. A	48. C	84. B	120. C
13. B	49. C	85. B	121. B
14. C	50. B	86. B	122. C
15. D	51. B	87. A	123. A
16. C	52. A	88. C	124. A
17. C	53. D	89. A	125. B
18. B	54. C	90. D	126. A
19. B	55. A	91. D	127. C
20. C	56. A	92. D	128. A
21. B	57. C	93. A	129. C
22. A	58. D	94. A	130. B
23. D	59. A	95. D	131. A
24. A	60. C	96. B	132. A
25. C	61. A	97. B	133. C
26. A	62. C	98. A	134. D
27. B	63. A	99. A	135. C
28. B	64. D	100. A	136. A
29. A	65. C	101. C	137. B
30. B	66. A	102. B	138. D
31. D	67. C	103. B	139. C
32. D	68. D	104. D	140. D
33. C	69. B	105. A	141. B
34. D	70. D	106. C	142. C
35. A	71. D	107. C	143. C
36. A	72. D	108. D	

Answers

Answers

Benchmark Test 1

1. C	18. A	35. D	52. C
2. C	19. A	36. B	53. D
3. B	20. B	37. C	54. B
4. C	21. D	38. A	55. D
5. B	22. D	39. B	56. D
6. A	23. D	40. D	57. A
7. D	24. C	41. C	58. B
8. D	25. B	42. B	59. B
9. A	26. B	43. A	60. B
10. B	27. A	44. A	61. C
11. C	28. B	45. B	62. B
12. A	29. B	46. C	63. C
13. A	30. A	47. B	64. C
14. D	31. B	48. C	65. B
15. D	32. A	49. A	66. A
16. C	33. A	50. A	67. D
17. B	34. C	51. D	68. C

Benchmark Test 2

1. C	15. D	29. A	43. C
2. B	16. B	30. A	44. A
3. D	17. C	31. B	45. B
4. D	18. A	32. D	46. D
5. B	19. B	33. D	47. D
6. B	20. C	34. A	48. B
7. D	21. D	35. C	49. C
8. B	22. A	36. B	50. C
9. C	23. C	37. D	51. B
10. A	24. B	38. B	52. C
11. C	25. B	39. D	53. A
12. B	26. C	40. A	54. A
13. D	27. A	41. B	55. C
14. B	28. B	42. C	

Benchmark Test 3

1. C	15. B	29. C	43. A
2. A	16. D	30. B	44. C
3. D	17. B	31. D	45. C
4. B	18. B	32. B	46. B
5. A	19. D	33. C	47. A
6. B	20. B	34. B	48. A
7. C	21. C	35. C	49. B
8. C	22. C	36. A	50. B
9. B	23. B	37. B	51. B
10. A	24. A	38. D	52. B
11. D	25. D	39. D	53. D
12. A	26. A	40. C	54. B
13. A	27. C	41. A	55. C
14. A	28. A	42. A	

Benchmark Test 4

1. A	17. B	33. A	49. D
2. D	18. D	34. D	50. B
3. A	19. B	35. A	51. C
4. D	20. B	36. A	52. B
5. A	21. C	37. B	53. C
6. B	22. A	38. B	54. C
7. C	23. D	39. C	55. D
8. D	24. B	40. A	56. B
9. C	25. B	41. B	57. A
10. A	26. D	42. B	58. B
11. B	27. D	43. C	59. B
12. C	28. C	44. D	60. D
13. B	29. C	45. A	61. C
14. D	30. A	46. B	62. C
15. B	31. C	47. C	
16. B	32. D	48. A	

Answers

Benchmark Test 5

1. D	14. C	27. B	40. D
2. C	15. C	28. B	41. C
3. A	16. D	29. C	42. B
4. C	17. C	30. C	43. C
5. D	18. D	31. C	44. B
6. B	19. D	32. B	45. C
7. A	20. B	33. B	46. D
8. B	21. C	34. D	47. D
9. A	22. B	35. A	48. A
10. B	23. D	36. B	49. B
11. A	24. B	37. D	50. D
12. D	25. C	38. B	51. D
13. D	26. D	39. B	52. B

Outcome Test

1. C	16. C	31. D	46. D
2. C	17. D	32. D	47. B
3. A	18. B	33. D	48. B
4. C	19. B	34. A	49. D
5. C	20. B	35. C	50. B
6. D	21. B	36. C	51. B
7. C	22. A	37. B	52. D
8. B	23. B	38. D	53. D
9. B	24. D	39. C	54. B
10. A	25. C	40. B	55. D
11. D	26. C	41. C	56. D
12. B	27. B	42. B	57. C
13. D	28. B	43. C	58. C
14. A	29. A	44. C	59. B
15. B	30. D	45. B	60. D

Practice Test 1

1. C	16. B	31. C	46. B
2. B	17. A	32. B	47. C
3. A	18. A	33. A	48. C
4. A	19. B	34. A	49. B
5. D	20. D	35. A	50. B
6. D	21. B	36. D	51. A
7. B	22. C	37. A	52. B
8. D	23. A	38. B	53. C
9. D	24. D	39. A	54. C
10. B	25. D	40. C	55. B
11. B	26. D	41. D	56. D
12. A	27. B	42. B	57. C
13. D	28. D	43. C	58. D
14. A	29. C	44. D	
15. A	30. B	45. D	

Practice Test 2

1. D	15. D	29. D	43. C
2. D	16. A	30. A	44. A
3. C	17. B	31. B	45. D
4. B	18. D	32. A	46. C
5. C	19. C	33. A	47. C
6. D	20. C	34. A	48. A
7. A	21. A	35. D	49. B
8. A	22. C	36. A	50. C
9. B	23. D	37. B	51. B
10. A	24. D	38. D	52. B
11. B	25. D	39. B	53. H
12. A	26. A	40. B	54. C
13. D	27. B	41. B	55. J
14. D	28. B	42. D	56. A

Answers

SAT II
Practice Test

1. D	11. E	21. E	31. E
2. A	12. A	22. D	32. B
3. D	13. C	23. A	33. C
4. A	14. C	24. C	34. A
5. E	15. A	25. C	35. E
6. A	16. E	26. D	36. B
7. B	17. C	27. B	37. B
8. E	18. C	28. A	38. D
9. C	19. D	29. D	39. C
10. A	20. A	30. D	40. A

ACT
Practice Test

1. C	11. D	21. D	31. D
2. G	12. H	22. F	32. H
3. C	13. C	23. B	33. B
4. G	14. H	24. H	34. G
5. A	15. A	25. C	35. B
6. J	16. H	26. A	36. H
7. A	17. C	27. F	37. C
8. G	18. J	28. D	38. J
9. C	19. A	29. H	39. A
10. F	20. G	30. G	40. H

Answers